RESPONSIVE AGILE COACHING

HOW TO ACCELERATE YOUR COACHING OUTCOMES WITH MEANINGFUL CONVERSATIONS

Niall McShane

ISBN: 978-19-5-036738-2

Published by

 LIFESTYLE
ENTREPRENEURS
P R E S S

If you are interested in publishing through Lifestyle Entrepreneurs Press, write to:
Publishing@LifestyleEntrepreneursPress.com

Publications or foreign rights acquisition of our catalog books.
Learn More: *www.LifestyleEntrepreneursPress.com*

Printed in the USA

CONTENTS

FOREWORD

For more than 25 years, I have been working in this system we call "agile." In the beginning, I was experimenting because everything was theoretical. Later, I was working on making these approaches solid and reliable and, most of all, delivering value to the client. What has always been a big question mark for me is the fact that although the results of agile implementation were initially successful, clients always had an excuse to step back into their old habits—the old habits that resulted in non-delivery.

Later on, I detected the power of old paradigms deeply embedded in the organizations, in areas such as decision making, documentation standards, career paths, bureaucracy, job descriptions, evaluation and reward, and—last but not least—habits. Habits, once in position, are difficult to change ("it does not work for us") and also define a person or company's reflexes under stress. These deeply rooted habits make it difficult to help people change; it is common for people and organizations to revert back to their old ways. People bump into an issue, and instead of fixing it in an agile way "forward," they regress "backward" by reimplementing old habits. This problem offered a massive opportunity: the professional domain of the agile coach.

Now there are a lot of people who call themselves agile coaches; however, and I am so sorry to say this, I often meet coaches who don't know how to coach. Agile knowledge and experience are often issues already, but the lack of coaching skills strikes me over and over again as a major problem within this professional domain.

The question is: what exactly are those coaching skills? I do not claim I have the one and only answer, but for me it is clear that "supporting people in finding their own way" is not the way. For me, an agile coach is like a sports coach. Sometimes you have to be directive and strict on the dos and don'ts, and sometimes you have to let teams struggle a bit and move forward on their own. Collective change (to achieve collective benefits) and tailor-made team improvements are both part of the support needed, and this is what the book is all about.

I recommend you read this book to learn. Read to see how this book can help you in your career. A professional agile coach is always interested in the lessons and improvements that can be learned from another. Enjoy!

Arie van Bennekum
(co-) Author of the Agile Manifesto

ABOUT THE AUTHOR

Before we go any further, let me answer your obvious question: "Why should I listen to you?"

My day job is hiring, training, and mentoring agile coaches whilst delivering agile coaching to a broad range of clients. I am a Professional Certified Coach accredited with the International Coaching Federation and I have a Masters of Business Administration. Of course, I've also gained certifications in scrum, scaling frameworks, human centered design and other industry qualifications as I moved through my career. You can check out my online profiles for more on my background.

But this book is *not* about what I've learned from studying agile; instead it mostly draws from my experiences on-the-job. Some of what you'll read in this book I learned as the head of an agile coach academy at a large (30,000 people) Australian corporate that was undergoing a full transformation in its way of working. Other content comes from my 10+ years of agile coaching across company-level initiatives as well as work at small companies with only three to four teams.

Prior to agile I was a professional leadership coach, and before that I was a professional sports coach (my first degree was in sports science), working with elite athletes up to the Olympic level. In short, I love coaching and I live agile.

The personal and spiritual life I lead has greatly influenced my work as a coach. I consider myself a practicing Buddhist and an amateur neuroscientist; both of these pursuits have been woven into this book alongside professional coaching and agile content. I'm not claiming to know everything about the topic of agile coaching, but what I can say is I've lived and practiced everything I write about in this book—and it works!

ACKNOWLEDGEMENTS

As I began to explore writing this book, I conducted a pre-order campaign to "crowdfund" and test the idea with the agile community. This book sold 312 copies before I'd written one word. I'd like to acknowledge these early "backers" of my idea and their contributions to bringing the project into reality. Here are all the wonderful people who signed up as contributors; thank you from the bottom of my heart. I couldn't have done this without your early support.

Arash Arabi

Beresford D'Silva

Brad Bennet

Chris Riley

Fiona Tibballs

Daniel Prager

Ian Main

John Farrow

Michael Law

Rasoul Baghdad

Ravi Shankar

Ross MacIntyre

Sandip Rananavare

Chelsea Bates (Adaptovate)

Paul McNamara (Adaptovate)

The Responsive Agile Coaching model draws upon elements from the work of Otto Scharmer and the Presencing Institute.[1] My ideas have come from experiencing workshops run out of MIT's u.lab online program that utilizes Theory U. You can go to the website to learn more: www.presencing.org.

I would like to acknowledge the book's cartoonist/illustrator, Simon Kneebone, who worked patiently to capture the style, look, and feel of what the Responsive Agile Coaching model aims to communicate. Thank you for your wonderful work.

HOW TO READ THIS BOOK

The best way to use this book is to consider it a laboratory book for you to use in order to design and conduct behavioral experiments (on yourself) as you practice coaching throughout your day. I suggest you keep an open journal or notebook, and as you read, stop and pause periodically to jot down ideas, insights, actions, opportunities, or experiments that you can execute as relevant coaching scenarios arise.

The practice of reading, understanding, then learning by doing experiments will greatly accelerate your ability to turn the theoretical concepts written here into practical capability uplift in your agile coaching.

Please note, some of the concepts in this book may seem very abstract, but within every chapter I'll provide you with practical experiments and actions you can take to solidify these concepts and build up learned experience, which will help you more deeply appreciate them.

The ideas in the book build on each other, so it is important that you read the chapters sequentially. I introduce language at the start of the book that I then expand on and utilize later, so you may get confused if you skip ahead.

In addition, I've created a community around the ideas in this book, so I recommend you join in and, as you read, participate in conversations with others who are also reading or have read the book. You can find the community at www.responsiveagile.coach

I hope you have as much joy reading this book as I did writing it!

PART I
WHY RESPONSIVE
AGILE COACHING?

Introduction

In Part 1, I want to give you a little background on agile and agile coaching as well as point out some of our industry's challenges that this book aims to address. I'll also share some personal stories that led me to write this book as well as start to outline the core elements of the Responsive Agile Coaching model.

CHAPTER 1.

THE AGILE INDUSTRY

The Rise of Agile Coaching

According to a recent article in *Forbes Magazine* by one of the world's leading thinkers in management, Steve Denning, "Agile is eating the world"—a bold statement.[2] Agile is a way of working, and to adopt this way of working, people are required to change their values, principles, and practices. This is where agile coaching comes in—to support people in changing their ways.

There's been a shift in how industry sees this move to agile; from it being primarily about agile process implementation to towards it being a change in mindset (values, attitudes, beliefs) across the workforce.

In large-scale transformations, agile coaching is now considered part of everyone's role. Like leadership being a distributed responsibility, agile coaching is being built into other positions, such as change managers, leaders, and other "agents of change." I believe it is time we reconsider agile coaching as a skill; it is time to encourage more people in a variety of roles to build their capability to deliver agile coaching. So, this book is about agile coaching and NOT just for those with the role of agile coach.

The subtitle of this book points to two key themes or consistent pain points in the agile coaching industry that I am attempting to solve for:

1. To be more effective and achieve coaching outcomes faster.
2. Reconnecting with the meaning of work.

Outcomes

Agile coaches are constantly under pressure to prove their worth and show value. Agile coaching engagements typically need to show observable improvements within 15 to 20 weeks (sometimes shorter); in this span of time, an agile coach is expected to make an impact, establish a system of work, or correct an "off-the-rails" project utilizing their skills. Coaches who do not have the ability to combine their hard (process) agile knowledge together with their softer (coaching) capability will struggle to effect change in these timeframes. This book is my contribution to help deliver coaching outcomes faster through enabling coaches to balance, in the moment, between how often they tell (the client what to do) and how much they ask clients open questions (e.g., "What do you think?").

If you're just starting out on your agile coaching career, this book will help guide you towards what you need to know to ensure you can build both your "agile" and "coaching" knowledge together as you progress through your career. If you're an experienced agile coach, this book will allow you to experiment with a new model of coaching that leverages the best of what you already know while supporting you to integrate deeper conversations into your practice. Regardless of your circumstance, this book will enable you to accelerate the delivery of coaching outcomes.

Meaning

Coaches are telling me that they want to conduct meaningful and impactful conversations to help their clients change their mindsets, beliefs, and attitudes relating to agile but don't know how. This lack of meaning at work is now seen as a global issue, with a recent survey of 2,285 professionals across 26 industries finding that employees crave more meaning.[3] The research findings were clear:

> *"Employees want more meaning from their work and are even willing to trade money to get it."*

What agile coaches need to know is that (almost) no other role has so much potential to bring meaning to the workplace than ours. As you read, you'll learn a new agile coaching model that enables you to conduct meaningful conversations that support clients to not only change their mindsets but also adopt new agile processes. By using this model, you will literally make meaning for yourself (and your clients) at work; it will feel good AND produce results/outcomes faster—a win-win!

CHAPTER 2.

THE STORY BEHIND THIS BOOK

The Agile Coaching Expert

I was walking out of an interview room when I turned to Sarah, who was helping me recruit agile coaches, and sighed. "That's another no..."

This was the thirteenth such interview, and an interesting pattern was emerging across all the applicants.

Before I tell you what this pattern was, let me give you a bit of background on the situation and the type of agile coach we were looking to hire. The agile coaches we were seeking required two key competencies. They needed to be able to:

- Work with, influence, and coach leaders in the adoption of agile.

- Advise and lead a team of agile coaches to implement changes to the way of working across a business function (large system of work).

Sound simple enough?

Now let's go back to the emerging pattern in the job applicants. What was becoming obvious after over a dozen interviews (screened from dozens of resumes) is that senior agile coaches were entirely ill-equipped to conduct coaching conversations with senior managers/executives.

Of course, we found a few applicants with the right stuff, but they were rare and the exception to the norm; maybe 5 percent. The "deal-breaker" question we would ask ourselves to determine whether the applicant should be given a senior agile coaching role was: "After the first meeting with an executive, would this agile coach be asked back for another conversation?" The answer kept coming back as an emphatic "NO!"

"Why?" I hear you asking. The answer is simple enough; senior agile coaches have traditionally been recognized and rewarded for their agile expertise. The coaching part of their agile coach role has not really been emphasized. Coaching for agile coaches usually means process coaching; providing advice on the best way to do something—tips, tricks, and shortcuts to a more efficient and effective way to work based on agile values, principles, and practices.

The problem I needed solving, though, was different to simply needing a coach to help with agile processes. I required agile coaches who had the capability to deal with resistance to change and situations where telling or even showing people what to do was not enough. I needed agile coaches who could, when required, hold back giving advice and stop being the agile expert. What I needed was a listener who could ask the right questions in order to help to influence beliefs, values, and attitudes; this "professional" type of coaching was vital, especially with executives. Upon reflection, I realized I wanted to hire coaches who could, in addition to being agile experts, bring a non-expert mind to their agile coaching; a mind that helps the people they're coaching to understand the emotions and beliefs that are blocking them from "getting on board" with the change to agile.

All the coaches we interviewed were specialists in agile processes; in fact, they were expert-level. But they were awful at putting their advice aside and working with the emotions, attitudes, values, and beliefs of the people they were coaching.

One example was when I asked one of the applicants this question:

> *"How would you use emotions*
> *as you work with clients?"*

Upon asking this question, the candidate got visibly annoyed with me and replied, "Well, that just sounds manipulative!" He refused to answer the question and was clearly uncomfortable with discussing emotions at all.

Now you could just dismiss this as us being overly picky or setting the bar too high or having a poorly worded job advert, but the gap was so clear relative to the applicants with the right stuff that the following statement was undeniable: *Most experienced agile coaches don't have the capability to discuss emotions, attitudes, beliefs, and values with their clients.*

What became obvious to me after conducting all these interviews and seeing this pattern repeatedly was that what was needed from agile coaches had changed and the coaches had not changed with this need. Agile coaches have to be able to *coach*; they need the ability to be a non-expert, ask questions instead of giving answers, work with emotions, and deal with human stuff—not just process.

When I saw all these expert coaches fail to meet my organization's needs, I empathized with these highly skilled, competent, and confident senior agile coaches. The emerging need for agile coaches to include other elements in addition to process implementation coaching had caught them out.

The Agile Coaching Beginner

At the same time as I was hiring for senior coaching roles, I was establishing a coaching academy with fifty internal trainee agile coaches. These people were invited to participate in a capability uplift initiative based on their mindsets, attitudes, and enthusiasm for learning.

So, on the one hand I could see the gap in the senior coaches being interviewed, while on the other hand I was working with fifty beginners at the start of their career journeys. I noticed a big difference between the expert agile coaches and the beginners.

The beginners were curious, they weren't full of advice, they listened deeply, and they sought to understand the person who was talking to them before offering an opinion. Expert coaches had lost these abilities.

I was training the beginners right at the start of their careers, explaining that they needed to understand the basics of coaching; this required them to (sometimes) hold back their opinions and leave room for those they were coaching to solve their own problems without being told the answer from an agile expert.

It was then that the idea for this book emerged. What if there was a way for agile coaches to develop into experts while retaining their ability to be open and curious as well as deeply listen to what the client needs? What if there were a model for agile coaching to help you choose how to best respond as either the agile expert or with a more open, non-expert mind?

Expert-Beginner Tension

So, what do the two above stories tell us about what great agile coaching looks like? The reason it has been so difficult to "nail down" what great agile coaching looks like is due to what I call expert-beginner tension. Agile coaching involves two almost opposing behaviors or forces that have confused our industry for years.

The first behavior is to act as a confident agile expert; giving advice on the technical or process aspects of adopting agile as a way to work. Easy, right? Well, it's the second behavior where a lot of the confusion arises; agile coaching also involves coaching people through change. To help people progress from one way of working to another involves softer skills; to execute these soft skills, the agile coach must be open-minded, listen deeply, and put aside their expertness (and act like a beginner). By taking on the mindset of a beginner, the coach is curious, which then makes room for deeper conversations, where the coach displays compassion and empathy for the client's situation. By assuming this beginner's mindset, the coach is better able to work with and support clients through the change. I'll expand on this idea of an expert and beginner tension in the next chapter, but for now, just realize that this tension is a positive and useful aspect which agile coaches need to work with.

Agile coaches have had no guidance on where and when to use these often-competing behaviors—until now. The Responsive Agile Coaching model will help you answer one of agile coaching's most perplexing questions: *"Do I tell the client what to do, or ask for their opinion and listen deeply to the answer?"*

The secret to this model is developing your ability to stop reacting and instead respond when called upon to coach. Let's quickly discuss that before getting into the rest of the book.

Responsive Coaching

I see the next "version" of agile coaching including the ability to choose how to respond when called upon to help. There will be times when clients need you to be the agile expert; this applies when you're faced with "just tell or show me what to do." There will also be times when the client needs you to be more like an open, curious beginner. This non-expert type of agile coaching is required when you are faced with "I'm not sure I need to be told what to do" or when you don't have all the answers. In this second example, agile coaching is about helping co-create the new way of working *with* the client as opposed to telling or showing them the what or how of agile.

Great agile coaches are responsive; they know when and how to shift their approach to serve their clients and get the results the organization is expecting from their work. I would even go further to say the truly masterful coaches can "dance in the moment" between these two extremes—at times, they give expert agile advice; then, the next moment, they deeply listen with non-judgmental awareness before asking an open question to help provoke thinking and introspection in the client.

I've witnessed these masterful coaches work, and when I first saw them in action, I thought it was magic; so incredible to watch. I could not fathom the skills required to, in one sentence, discuss a highly complex process used to manage a portfolio of work and then, in the very next moment, help a leader deeply consider their impact on workplace culture. This is what responsive agile coaching looks like, and this is what I want you to be able to do through reading and implementing the ideas in this book. You'll get results from your coaching in days, not weeks, because you will have developed your ability to *respond*—not react—when called upon to help your clients. By being able to respond as you deliver coaching, you are more likely to take the right approach (at the right time) and get to the outcome faster. Let me show you how!

CHAPTER 3.

THE AGILE COACH AND AGILE COACHING

I t is really important for us to be on the same page about what agile coaching is and what an agile coach does. Even if you've been working this role for many years, it is still helpful to establish concrete definitions and get some of the language straight before we proceed further.

Definitions

By "agile coach" I am referring to anyone who is or aspires to deliver agile coaching, irrespective of their actual job role or title. So, if you're a leader, manager, agile practitioner, or even a professional agile coach, I am using this term generally.

Also, throughout the book I'll refer to "clients." By client I mean any individual or team you are coaching; so from here onward, you can assume the word refers to either.

Now that we have those two terms out of the way, it is important to get a clear answer for this simple question: "What is agile coaching?"

One of the problems with defining agile coaching right now is that when you ask 10 people this question, you get 15 different answers. So, I'm going to give you my very simple definition to get us going:

> *Agile coaching is enabling others to adopt agile ways of working.*

I like this definition because the outcome is observable; people are either working differently or they aren't. This definition may seem simple enough, but it is important to clarify what the "coaching" part of agile coaching actually means, as well as what "agile" means in this context. We have sports coaches, life coaches, leadership coaches, and many other types of coaches, which creates confusion in the agile coaching community. So, to clear up any uncertainty, I want to explain agile coaching by considering the two parts "agile" and "coaching" separately.

The "Agile" Part of Agile Coaching

In any workplace, individual people will work with others, follow processes, and utilize various tools to get their work done. Let's call this a "system of work." The agile coach has the job of helping the people in this system to change the way they get their work done; to adopt better ways of working.

For any workplace adopting agile, there are associated frameworks, values, principles, processes, roles, patterns, tools, practices, ceremonies, naming conventions, methods, models, etc. Agile practitioners and consultants need to not only have knowledge of these as part of their role but are also expected to have experience in actually doing them and implementing them into how people work.

Agile coaching is usually about implementing a practice and its associated processes. Sure, these are underpinned by agile values and principles, but the coach's primary outcome is to enable the adoption of the new ways of working (processes), resulting in observable behavioral change.

Agile coaches need to understand the types of agile frameworks (collections of processes, roles, and associated artifacts) that apply to the size of the system of work they are coaching.

I typically see three main sizes for systems of work that agile coaches operate in: team-level (small; up to 30 people), teams of teams (medium; 31 – 300 people), and large systems (301 – 1300 people). This is discussed in more detail in chapter 20; for now, this is just context regarding the role itself.

Agile coaches should have experience *doing* a specific agile process (run a planning session or facilitate a retrospective) before they consider helping others adopt it. For example, before considering oneself an agile coach, an agile practitioner should have experience in executing (doing) all team-level agile practices using one or multiple frameworks for at least six months. In other words, before you coach an agile practice, you need to have actually done it yourself. This applies to each size system of work; only coach that which you have done. If an agile coach has not personally done the practices they're attempting to coach others to do, they come across as inauthentic and are usually met with skepticism. So, good agile coaches come with lots of experience; they've been there and done it; hence, they can coach it.

To summarize, agile coaches need to know and have practiced the appropriate frameworks for the size of the system of work they are coaching. I recommend a progressive, three-step sequence for agile coaches to follow when they are learning new knowledge/skills relating to agile ways of working: (Make sure you) KNOW IT – (and can) DO IT – (then) TEACH IT.

I will talk a lot more about this later, but I think you get the idea; if you think you are ready to be an agile coach on a topic, then you'd better have the knowledge, have applied it with real teams, and be able to prove you have the right depth of understanding by teaching someone else. Only then are you ready to coach the topic.

Of course, a progressive sequence is not meant to always be linear in how it actually happens; coaches often learn by doing a practice first, then read the theory later, and that's OK. However, coaching capability in a particular area should be built upon knowledge and experience.

The "Coaching" Part of Agile Coaching

The type of coaching I've referred to so far is called "process" coaching. There's another type of coaching that is part of the agile coach's role: "professional" coaching. This type of coaching is required in situations when simply telling or showing people how to do agile won't work. This usually occurs when people are resistant to the proposed changes or the coach needs to co-create the way of working with their clients. The International Coaching Federation describes professional coaching as *"partnering with clients in a thought-provoking and creative process that inspires them to maximize their personal and professional potential."* [4]

During a professional coaching conversation, the coach co-creates and inspires the client through deep listening and powerful questions. Note: professional coaching is not about giving advice (providing answers) on agile processes. Professional coaching is completely different to process coaching; almost the opposite, in fact. Process coaching gives answers on how to work, whereas professional coaching asks questions to understand why we work.

Although professional coaching has been included in some recent agile coaching competency frameworks, I would argue it does not naturally fit into a day-in-the-life of an agile coach, at least in the way it is taught as part of traditional certified professional coaching courses. A professional coach formalizes the coaching relationship (time, duration, often even the number of sessions) upfront when working with a client and does so in a structured, orderly format.

Rarely do agile coaches sit down deliberately and use a structured format when conducting "coaching" conversations. And rarely would an agile coach conduct a considered and structured deep coaching conversation on the reasons why their clients work the way they do (which is how professional coaching is conducted). Of course, some of this type of coaching does happen, but it is not the norm. Despite professional coaching not fitting neatly into an agile coach's day, there are certain elements from professional coaching (listening, use of questions, silence) that are vital to becoming a great agile coach.

Agile coaches need professional coaching capabilities but do not use them in the way they are currently taught. I'll expand on this later, showing how and when agile coaches should use professional coaching techniques.

Chapter Summary

- Agile coaching is not only a role but a capability, defined as a type of coaching that enables others to adopt agile ways of working.

- Agile coaches need to know and have done agile prior to attempting to coach others.

- Agile coaching involves two often opposing types of coaching—agile process coaching and professional coaching. The latter is not well understood or commonly practiced by agile coaches.

References and Further Reading

1. This book builds on the work from Otto Scharmer and the Presencing Institute: www.Presencing.org.
2. Stephen Denning, "Why Agile is Eating the World," *Forbes*, January 2, 2018, www.Forbes.com.
3. Andrew Reece, Gabriella Kellerman, Alexi Robichaux, www.BetterUp.com, "BETTERUP // MEANING AND PURPOSE AT WORK."
4. https://coachfederation.org/faqs.

5. Stephen Denning, *The Age of Agile: How Smart Companies Are Transforming the Way Work Gets Done*, (HarperCollins Focus: 2018).

6. Otto Scharmer, *Theory U: Leading from the Future as It Emerges*, (Berrett-Koehler: 2007).

7. If you really want to know my inspiration for this chapter, here's a Buddhist book that started it all for me: Shun-ryu Suzuki, *ZEN Mind Beginner's Mind*, (Shambhala Library: 2006).

8. Go to www.responsiveagile.coach to learn with others who have read or are reading this book; you can also visit www.responsiveagilecoaching.com for up-to-date content, downloads, and templates.

PART II
WHAT IS THE RESPONSIVE AGILE COACHING MODEL?

Introduction

In Part II, I'm going to slowly build up the elements of the Responsive Agile Coaching model for you, piece by piece. Once you thoroughly understand the model, I will then go through and show you exactly how to use it. What's really exciting about the Responsive Agile Coaching model is that for the first time it unpacks and provides specific, detailed guidelines on how to actually conduct an agile coaching conversation with a client. The model is going to introduce some new language to describe how agile coaching works, which may seem strange or a little unusual, but it is necessary because we need to reframe what agile coaching is and how it's delivered.

CHAPTER 4.

TWO STORIES EXPLAIN HOW THE MODEL ORIGINATED

I want to take you through the two scenarios I see over and over as I mentor agile coaches through their careers. In one scenario, the coach has the answer and provides a solution, and the experience feels gratifying. In the second scenario, the coach's solution is NOT the answer; this is where a lot of coaches struggle, give up, or go and coach somewhere else. The model I've developed provides for a response in both scenarios and gives coaches a means to deal with both situations.

Below I'll tell two stories based on both scenarios, then I'll introduce the Responsive Agile Coaching model and explain it in detail.

The first story is what I call a "sunny-day scenario," meaning everything goes according to the script; the coach plays the expert and the client plays the student who accepts the wisdom provided by the coach. Everyone in this scenario walks away with what they came for.

Sunny-Day Story

Let me tell you a story that's happening now, as I write this book. It is about a coaching engagement I have just commenced over the last two weeks. It is a great example of when an agile coach gets a "clean run" to deliver their services into an organization, meeting little resistance to change. A nice "sunny-day" scenario.

The client has a problem project. It has been running for a year, is behind schedule, and the team has a lot of internal conflict. Management feels the project is not well governed and is concerned about the risk of further delays. I'm hired as the agile coach to stabilize the project, organize the way of working, and improve the team culture. Here's a quote from my first meeting with the product owner (Fred).

"I think we need to reduce the number of agile ceremonies; they're a waste of my time," Fred says. He stops talking and sits back in his chair with a posture that says, "I've had enough".

I think to myself, *Wow, this guy really is frustrated; he seems to really care but is fed up with the team.*

This is normal team-level agile coaching—nothing special going on here—but you may be thinking, *Is this a sunny-day scenario?* The answer is yes, and you'll see why as our story continues.

In this first meeting, I made sure the complaining product owner felt heard. I didn't argue or interrogate his claims and mostly listened and empathized. Over the next week, I met with the team and project manager and learned the following:

- The product owner has everyone fearful of speaking up.
- The project has no governance approach.
- Basic team-level agile practices are not in place.
- The team does not have a social contract.
- Retrospectives are superficial and not getting to the root cause of problems.

I meet with my sponsor, Mark, to discuss the plan of action. "OK, Niall, what is the plan here?" Mark enquires.

"We need to bring order to the team's way of working; it is chaos at the moment. The easiest way to do this is just to go back to the basics of the scrum framework. Then once these are in place, I'll work with the individual people on their attitudes, values, behaviors," I reply.

"OK, what changes are you going to implement first?" Mark asks. "I really need this project to have better governance; the board needs to know when it will be delivered. Whatever you want to do, I am fully behind you to implement your recommendations."

After this meeting, I began telling and showing the team how to set up a more formalized scrum implementation. The team recognized me as an expert-level coach, I did not meet any resistance to my suggestions (even the PO did as I asked), and my sponsor ensured I could just get on with implementing change.

Over the following two weeks, I then started on the "softer" aspects of coaching: a social contract creation workshop and a deep retro to air all grievances. I worked one-on-one with the PO, and the team started to learn how to have open and honest conversations about their behavior.

All of my recommendations were accepted and implemented, and within two sprints, the team's ceremonies were completely in line with what would be considered a standard implementation of scrum. I did this by stepping in and facilitating all ceremonies and helping reconfigure the team's tooling setup. I either did it myself or told others to do it for me. There was little discussion or negotiation on what I was suggesting. The sponsor was happy, the team was comfortable with me telling them what to do, and the results came quickly.

See the illustration below for a visual representation of this coaching process; a clear, straight pathway to executing my role as an agile coach.

Sunny-Day Story Debrief

So, what happened in this scenario? Let's debrief.

Nothing out of the ordinary here; this is traditional agile coaching. I was able to do my job because a few prerequisites were in place that allowed for a sunny-day coaching scenario:

+ Sponsorship and permission to coach.
+ A clear reason for me to be there; a well-defined urgent problem that required attention.
+ I had the right skills and experience to undertake the job I was being asked to do.

This coaching engagement went "to plan" because all these pre-requisites were in place. Let's look at each one.

Firstly, I could go in to work with the team, knowing I had sponsorship to challenge the current way of working. You could call this power, support, or a mandate, but it all means the same thing: you can assertively implement suggestions by telling or showing people what to do. I didn't need to obtain permission per se because it is explicit that I'm here to change things. The team knows I'm sponsored, they know the organization is expecting change, and they know they need to at least give me an opportunity and listen.

Secondly, there were obvious issues/problems that required resolution. An experienced coach will see these immediately and quickly formulate ideas on how they should be solved.

Lastly, the coach has been in this situation before and has the learned experience of what to do and the advice the team needs to hear. Very quickly they can give answers and provide hands-on help and solutions.

Sunny-day coaching is the predominant approach agile coaches take and is what agile coaches are most known for. The client learns a new skill by the coach telling and then showing them the what and how of agile before embedding the new way of working and letting the client do it themselves. Writing a book about the above scenario, while useful, does not provide the agile coach with the complete picture. What happens when the coach meets resistance, either open or passive, to what they are proposing? The fifty beginner agile coaches I recently trained were not prepared for situations that didn't follow the approach outlined in the sunny-day scenario. That's when I started to see the need to provide coaches with guidance on what to do on "rainy days"; when they are not being listened to, are not well-sponsored, or don't have all the answers to the problems they're trying to solve.

Rainy-day coaching is quite different from sunny-day coaching, and it is not something well catered for within existing education or accreditation training programs for agile coaches. In rainy-day situations, simply telling or showing the client won't work; the answer is not obvious, and a different approach is required. Here's a real (and typical) rainy-day situation I experienced.

Rainy-Day Story

Jen was frustrated. She'd heard about how agile coaching of technology teams was "different" to coaching business teams, but the resistance to change she was experiencing was much higher than she expected. Jen's background as a change management specialist had brought her to agile coaching. She had learned the processes and practices of agile and was quite proficient as a facilitator, but coming into the technology department as an agile coach for the first time meant she was never going to be as knowledgeable about IT as the people she was coaching—no matter how much she read up.

Over her morning cup of coffee, Jen considered her day ahead; she was reflecting on a conversation she had the day prior with John, one of the technology team product owners.

"Hi, John. My name is Jen. I've been assigned to support you as your agile coach. How's it going?"

"Hey, Jen. What's up? Great to have another pair of hands to help get stuff done. What's your background?" John asked.

"I've just finished working on a project in our human resource department where I was helping implement agile across a few teams; my background is in leadership and culture."

Jen noticed that John's posture and mood changed quite rapidly; he didn't look as happy as he did five seconds before. "No offense, Jen, but you've got to be kidding me! Why would I be assigned a business coach to help me with my IT delivery team; this is ridiculous."

With that John walked off, leaving Jen stunned and confused.

Jen was now frustrated; her agile coaching career had been mostly smooth sailing to date, with only a few bumps of resistance along the way. She considered her next steps, jotting down options for a possible way forward on her notepad:

1. Find a way to "restart" the conversation.
2. Have a deeper conversation with John about his reaction; see what's under that.
3. Position my coach role as an enabler to solve his problems.
4. Find out what his problems are.

Jen headed into work with a mini plan. She met John at the elevator.

"Hi, John, I—"

John cut her off. "Sorry to interrupt you, Jen. I just wanted to apologize for yesterday. I'm not sure you're going to be a fit for what we need here. We've got so much backlogged work and not a lot of time. I just don't want to waste your time and mine when you aren't a technology expert."

Jen took a deep breath and relaxed her posture. In that moment, she made a purposeful attempt to empathize with John's situation before responding. "I get it, John. I really do. I'm not an IT specialist and I won't stand here and pretend that I am. What if I just observed for a few days? I'll stay out your way and won't take any of your time. After that we can talk, and if we both agree there's no value in me being around, then I'll talk to my manager. Would that be OK?"

"Yeah, I suppose, but please don't interfere with the team's work," John said.

"Sure, it's a deal; I'll put some time in your diary for Wednesday for us to debrief in three days; in the meantime, I'll observe."

Three days later, Jen and John were sitting in a meeting room for the debrief.

Jen opened the meeting. "Hi, John. I'd like to use this time to discuss your team's way of working but more specifically to check in with you and see how you're doing."

"Well, we're doing OK; the team had a great sprint, and we delivered on our goal—"

Jen politely interjected. "Sorry, John, to interrupt, but I just want to point out that you're talking about 'we,' your team. I asked how '*you*' are doing."

"Oh, well, yes. Umm…" John paused; there was silence.

Jen waited, listened, and watched intently. She put down her pen, straightened in her chair, leaned in slightly, and put both hands on the table and relaxed, signaling "I'm open to whatever you say next, without judgement."

John laughed nervously. "It's just funny—no one has ever really asks me how I'm doing, at least not the way you did. Everyone around here is so busy that checking in with how people are *really* doing just doesn't happen."

Jen didn't respond. She just kept listening, waiting for John, who looked like he had more to say.

"So, what did you observe over the last two days, Jen?"

"I observed busyness, pressure to deliver. I witnessed you running around, attempting to meet everybody else's expectations and keep the team productive as well as protected. I saw you, a product owner, who cares about his team and also cares about quality," Jen responded.

John laughed, less nervously this time. "Yep, that about sums it up. I guess you now see why I reacted when you came to me but were not going to help as a technical expert."

"John, agile coaches can do many things to help product owners; sure, there are the agile expert and technical expert parts of the role, but there's also the coach part, and that is where I think I can be of most use to you and your team. There are things I can implement to help with the busyness and pressure you're experiencing. As your coach, we can partner to protect your team while getting things done. I can put things in place with you and your scrum master to take the pressure off you." Jen said, then she was quiet.

John considered what Jen had said. "So you'd work *with* me?"

"Yes, I call it co-creating *your* way of working. That's how I roll, John; I do my job *with* others not *to* them; that way you own the way of working because you helped create it," Jen responded.

"OK, let's see how this goes. We can assess how we go every retro with the team," John agreed.

"Great, John, and thanks for hearing me out. So just to confirm and check: We're going to work together to implement changes and improve the team's way of working. We're a team on this, yes?"

"Yes, Jen. All good. I might even pick your brain on how I can manage my time a bit better."

As Jen left the meeting room, She reflected on the conversation and thought back to her coaching training. She sat down and quickly drew the model she'd utilized in the conversation with John in her notebook; she didn't want to forget the approach and wanted to keep it for future reference.

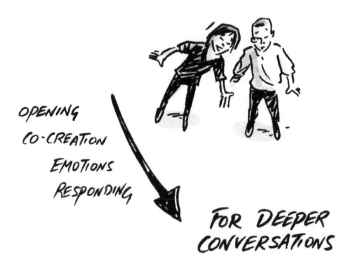

OPENING
CO-CREATION
EMOTIONS
RESPONDING

FOR DEEPER
CONVERSATIONS

Rainy-Day Story Debrief

Jen encountered resistance; simply telling or showing John the answer was not going to work. She had no opportunity to come in and implement changes to the way of working. She was not invited in to help the team change their practices. Jen started her coaching engagement in the same manner as the sunny-day scenario; she initiated the relationship but then had to have a reset.

The difference in this scenario was Jen had to take an alternate approach to see what was underneath the tip of the iceberg. It follows a downward pathway; let me explain what I mean by downward.

When people behave in an observable way, there are unseen factors at play. A person's beliefs and values underpin their attitudes and behaviors. When these unseen factors are challenged, the person can become emotional and react as John did when Jen asked for his time. What Jen did was in some way at odds to John's values or beliefs. For example, it is not unreasonable to think that John believes only technology professionals have the right to advise him on how they should work. John may also consider Jen's request disrespectful of his time, which he did not have a lot of. Ultimately, we will never know what it was that caused John to act the way he did, and it doesn't really matter. All Jen can do is change her approach—*respond* to the situation—which she did.

When Jen sat down with John the second time, she wasn't there to bring answers, solve agile problems, or show the team how to do agile better. Her approach represents a coaching model that follows a different pathway—one that is used when a deeper consideration of what's causing resistance is required.

Jen used listening, silence, and open questions to slow down the conversation. She saw John's problems with fresh (non-expert) eyes and empathized with his emotions. This allowed John to "feel felt"; it's where the coach and client both start to "let go" of their opinions and make room for new shared ones with neither trying to drive their agenda. John only did this when Jen's response to his question on what she had observed "hit the mark" and resonated with him. When John felt heard and understood, he then gave Jen the benefit of the doubt.

In conversations like these, there are always turning points; Jen sat quietly awaiting what was about to come. It's the moment when new things can emerge—ideas, options, relationships, or ways forward. It's after this turning point that co-creation starts, and John agrees that they can partner to "do it together." They leave the meeting with a very different relationship than they had prior. The two parties have let go of their old thinking and opinions and created a partnership to improve the team's way of working. The final step is embedding the new system, which in this instance is simply them working together. Jen confirmed and embedded this agreement prior to finalizing the meeting.

We'll refer back to this process in much more detail in the next and subsequent chapters.

The secret to great agile coaching is being able to respond to a coaching request or opportunity by either providing the answer or co-creating it with the client. A responsive agile coach executes whichever approach is necessary and required in the moment. Read on to see how these two response options interact to form the overall model for Responsive Agile Coaching.

Chapter Summary

- As an agile coach, sometimes you will have the answer to your client's questions, and sometimes your answer is either not accepted or is insufficient to solve the current problem.

- Being responsive simply means the agile coach is aware they have a choice between the two different pathways a conversation can follow.

CHAPTER 5.

TWO PATHWAYS, FOUR MOVES, ONE END POINT

Two Conversation Pathways

If we combine the two pictures from the sunny-day and rainy-day scenarios, we start to see the two pathways an agile coaching conversation can go down. More than 15 years of research from The Presencing Institute supports this pathway model, which is underpinned by "Theory U" and the work of Otto Scharmer at MIT.[2] The Responsive Agile Coaching model takes Theory U and applies it into the domain of agile coaching conversations. For the sake of simplicity, I'm going to refer to the first pathway as the "across" pathway and the second pathway as the "down" pathway.

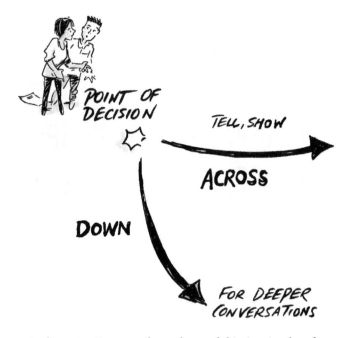

At this stage I want to keep the model in its simplest form to highlight the moment when the coach reaches a point of decision; a moment where they can make a choice and hopefully respond to what will best serve the client by choosing the appropriate pathway. Each pathway has what I'm going to call a move or series of moves associated with it. Let me take you through what I mean by the word "move," as this is new language and a new concept in agile coaching.

Overview of the Four Moves

The Responsive Agile Coaching model is a flow-based approach to conducting agile coaching conversations. The model is composed of four moves, which will help organize the rest of the book and all the associated concepts. I've used the word "moves" on purpose because each one involves two steps; actions where the coach does something.

Moves are not static but collectively combine to form the flow of an agile coaching conversation; here are the four moves:

1. **Sense then Respond** to what the client needs.
2. **Tell or Show** clients how to apply agile.
3. **Open and Hold** the space for deeper conversations.
4. **Await then Co-create** new ways of working.

The last element of the model is an end point, which is made up of a single step—to **Embed** the change as a better way to work.

The four moves together with the two conversation pathways help agile coaches navigate conversations to the end point. In the "across" pathway, the coach will *Tell or Show* the client how to do agile. The "down" pathway involves deeper conversations where the coach will *Open and Hold* the space to support clients to enter into a dialogue with the coach. Once in the Open and Hold move, the coach will then *Await* for emerging ideas before moving to *Co-create* the new ways of working with the client. Prior to choosing a pathway, the agile coach *Senses* there is a coaching moment, considers what will best serve the client and the situation, and then *Responds* accordingly.

Here's a simple version of the model to get us started; I'll fill in more detail as we progress through the book.

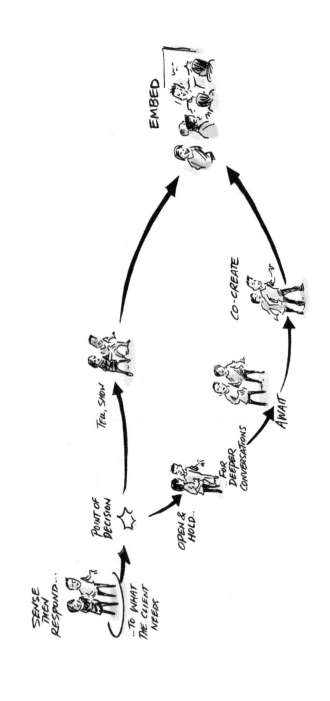

Let's take a bit of time now to explain each of the steps within each move. At this stage I want you to get the general concepts; these will come to life later when I show you how to actually conduct an agile coaching conversation using the model.

Move 1: Sense Then Respond

Agile coaching conversations are preceded by a series of events and activities involving the coach becoming aware that they are "on" and it is time for them to do their job as a coach. The coach is sensing the environment, looking for signals, or simply waiting to be asked for help; once this happens and an opportunity presents itself, a response may be required.

It is this ability to respond and not react that is central to the Responsive Agile Coaching model. To not act out of habit but consciously choose what to do (or not do) when called upon to help is the sign that responsive agile coaching is taking place. As you can see in the model, the Sense then Respond move finishes at a moment of choice: the responsive moment. Before we discuss this moment, let's dive deeper into each of the steps in this move.

Sense

Sensing your environment for the "moments that matter," where you can step up and play the role of an agile coach, is an important capability because without it, coaching conversations will not start. To master agile coaching, requires plenty of practice, and without well-honed sensing capability, you will miss your chance to start conversations with clients. This might sound obvious, but it is not; many coaches do not speak up when they should or fail to see an opportunity to coach—usually because they're not paying attention.

I suggest using the practices of mindfulness and listening to maintain a keen awareness of your environment (you'll learn about these in Part IV); by doing this you will start to see all the opportunities to deliver agile coaching. Also, as you become more experienced, you will know where and when agile coaching opportunities are most likely to arise. For example, experienced coaches know that walking out of a meeting to the elevator is a great opportunity to start a corridor coaching conversation with a senior leader who is rushing to their next meeting.

One word of advice when sensing: don't just look for facts and process data. Sensing also includes being on the lookout for other less obvious signals coming from the people around you; posture, tone of voice, or emotions can all be signs that there may be an unanswered question that nobody is asking.

Remember, in the sensing part of "Sense and Respond," we are only noticing what our senses are telling us, registering the data coming to us from our environment. We are not reacting or doing anything yet; jumping to "doing" too quickly reduces your ability to respond.

Finally, before I speak to the next step of this move, I want to recognize intuition. If you sense intuitively that something is happening, then give this your attention; do not dismiss it. Recently I was facilitating a group of 15 experienced agile practitioners. The subject was how to develop a psychologically safe environment. I heard someone say quietly to another participant: *"We should do an exercise on how to actually build safety."* I almost dismissed this statement, but I paused and was silent as the whole class waited for about 60 seconds as I considered what my intuition was trying to tell me. My inner voice said something like, "Niall, this is important; you should do as he says and work through the topic with the group." Of course, it was exactly what they needed and was the turning point in the three-day workshop where we took the conversation towards topics that needed to be discussed. My point is that I sensed using what I heard, but it was my intuition that made me pause and consider how best to respond.

Sensing: Practical Tips and an Experiment

In this multi-tasking world riddled with distractions, it is becoming more and more difficult to remain focused, mindful, and properly sense our environment, especially if we are coaching remotely/virtually.

I suggest you practice being sensitive to where you are and refrain from multi-taking as you coach. Be open to receiving and actively look for "weak" or small signals that could provide you with extra data or context about what's happening in your team. Stay open, listen, watch, and use all your senses to seek opportunities to coach.

Learn to listen, really, deeply listen; practice paying full attention to someone talking with you. Orient your mind to eagerly await what they're about to say; be genuinely curious when listening, and you will start to sense more, much more, in your conversations and environment. Keep a journal of how often you listen without judgment. I'll talk in detail about the practice of listening in Part IV.

Use mindfulness and listening to hone this capability. Keep a record in your journal of what happened when you followed a weak signal; run experiments to follow your intuition more and record results.

Try this experiment:

As you are coaching an individual or team, when you see an opportunity to improve their way of working, resist the urge to suggest a change or provide advice, instead you will keep sensing and observing, collect more data, and further understand the situation.

The Responsive Moment

After Sensing, we can Respond with an agile coaching conversation that follows one of two pathways represented by the two moves: "Tell or Show" or "Open and Hold." This is where the ability to respond comes from in the model—choosing which pathway best serves the client and the circumstances.

This is a critical moment that matters for the subsequent agile coaching conversation. A lot of coaches miss this moment; they fail to see it as an opportunity to intentionally guide the conversation along a pathway most suitable for the situation.

Knowing that this moment actually exists is the first step for most coaches. I encourage agile coaches to start to notice this moment. Often just being on the lookout for this responsive moment is enough to completely shift how an agile coach delivers coaching to clients.

To help you understand this moment, I'd like to share a personal story, which involves me missing this moment and not fully taking advantage of a coaching opportunity.

I was invited to come and "drop in" to a scrum master training course. At the time, I was the head of a coaching academy in a large corporation; I was the "head coach" for want of a better term. I walked into a class full of learners and was immediately put on the spot to answer a tricky question that had been put in the "parking lot" by the instructor. Jacqui, the instructor, turned to me as I entered the room. "Niall, it is great you are here. We've just been discussing a question to which I'm struggling to provide an answer; maybe you can help?" Everyone looked at me expectantly.

"Sure, no problem." I said confidently, my ego ensuring I projected confidence.

Jacqui posed the question: "So, Niall, we were wondering how to manage risks with scrum; our ex-project managers are confused."

Without thinking for even one second, I fired back an answer: "Risks are factored in as part of your estimates for product backlog items, and anyway, you only carry risk for a maximum of two weeks (a sprint)." I then walked away, feeling very smug with a little hit of endorphins that reinforced my expertness.

You might be reading this and thinking, *That sounds like a good answer.* That's not the point. I know that I could have helped everyone more if I'd taken a minute to understand what exactly the issue for the project managers regarding risks in scrum was. I played the role of the super-expert and upon reflection was very disappointed in my reaction and lack of response. I didn't even notice I was at a moment of choice.

Right, now let me get down to explaining more about the responsive moment. Assuming you do notice that you're at the "responsive moment," you can guide the conversation either across or down. "Tell or Show" moves the conversation *across* whereas "Open and Hold" moves the conversation *down.* The responsive agile coach will choose which move best serves the client and circumstance; that's what responsive means—a conscious decision to go across or down in the flow of conversation.

Respond

The best coaches appear to react in the moment, instantly utilizing their extensive experience; however my most amazing coaching interventions have always come from a considered response, *not* a reactive one. Never be afraid of taking a moment to consider what to do next. I believe the modern workplace values speed over consideration, but coaches should not prioritize speed as a key performance indicator; we're not computers. Getting to the wrong answer fast still results in a bad outcome.

Often after a busy day at work, when your mind is quiet, you'll find an answer to a problem or see a situation in a different light, and a great solution will arise; unfortunately, this often happens after the fact—when your perfect solution is no longer required. The coaching moment has passed. One aspect of responsive agile coaching is the ability to keep your head when everyone else is losing theirs, allowing you to consider the situation and then respond. Thinking of the answer after the coaching moment has passed can be frustrating, but see this as your performance indicator—your ability to offer coaching advice when it matters most (in the moment).

This ability to respond to client problems in real time is central and critical to the Responsive Agile Coaching model. In order to build your ability to be responsive in the moment, there's usually an amount of unlearning to do. Reacting habitually is the biggest barrier to developing this capability, but there are things you can do to develop this step. Start by slowing down. Pausing before acting may sound simple, but in the fast-paced world we work in, not having the answer immediately is sometimes looked upon unfavorably or, worse, judged as underperformance. So, you'll need to practice using mindfulness or a simple routine to help insert a pause between the "juicy agile problems" you're given and your habitual reaction to be the expert who can quickly offer an answer.

Respond: Practical Tips and an Experiment

One simple method to build up your respond capability is "intent for the day."

By reflecting daily and journaling on how you responded in certain situations or coaching conversations, you will start to bring awareness to how often you are responding versus reacting habitually. The key here is paying attention.

Controlling your urges is the key to responding as an agile coach. Start to notice your urges, habits, and reactions and then do not let them control you; instead, respond and control what you do or say.

Choose a regular team coaching situation and focus on it with intent before each workday begins. Notice when you react to triggers (usually you'll notice afterwards). Triggers are simply events or circumstances that start an automatic behavioral routine to run inside *you*. An example of a trigger could be when you are driving a car in busy traffic and have to change lanes (trigger); you then run a routine to indicate, check your mirrors and turn the steering wheel. Triggers are your normal, so spotting them can be difficult if you don't notice on purpose. That is why using a journal to record when you are responding in place of reacting is recommended. Using a journal will build your capability through simple observation. Also, keep track of your ability to coach in the moment that matters (and when you miss the opportunity), then try to take advantage of more opportunities.

Try this experiment:

When you are coaching an individual or team, and see an opportunity to improve their way of working, pause and notice the urge you have to implement a change or provide advice, instead of reacting habitually to the urge and instantly providing advice.

Move 2: Tell or Show

Telling or showing a client what to do is the typical move in agile coaching. This represents the majority of agile coaching work I see being delivered in organizations, which is OK and is appropriate most of the time. I see the average agile coach habitually react by telling or showing their clients agile. The difference between typical and responsive agile coaching conversations is that in a responsive conversation the coach makes this move as a conscious choice and after consideration as to whether it best serves the client, the situation, and the organization.

Tell

First of all, let's get something out of the way; most people don't like being told what to do. So, to ensure you, as the coach, have the right state of mind, I recommend you tell only after strongly orienting your mindset to "serve the client."

I often make a joke when mentoring agile coaches, referring to the tools they have in their agile "bag of tricks." I say to them, when they are out in the business working, do not "go around hitting everyone over the head with your agile hammer." In other words, try not to be the agile police who enforces the laws of agile by *telling* all the time (fyi, there are no laws of agile; I made that up).

Secondly, in order to Tell someone an answer to their agile problem, the agile coach needs to have appropriate knowledge and experience. Coaches who fake their knowledge when they Tell clients answers to agile problems are one of the most systemic challenges in our profession. Equally as bad are agile coaches with little knowledge who act like they know everything. So please, before you respond with the Tell step, ensure you are providing knowledge and expertise in line with your experience and don't overstate your confidence in your own opinion; have some humility.

One of the phrases I always cringe when I hear is: "*That's not agile!*" This statement highlights the biggest risk to building your "Tell" capability: becoming a dogmatic agile subject matter expert with an overemphasis on process implementation. The Responsive Agile Coaching model the way I mitigate this risk, as it provides alternatives to just telling people what to do; of course, sometimes it's required, so let me outline the best way to Tell.

The secret to "telling" is recognizing **how** and **when** to do so. When discussing how to use the Tell step, a lot can be summarized as what I would call consulting skills. Building rapport, managing personalities, influencing, and dealing with complexity are all part of a consultant's job. This book is not about consulting, so I am not going into detail on these topics and instead will focus on a few key tips on how an agile coach could execute the "Tell" step.

A simple and easy way to "soften" how you tell people is to offer advice rather than impose your opinions onto people. Of course, there will be times when a firmer hand is required, and you will need to be explicit; this is especially important with new-to-agile teams and when problems are pressing. So, I recommend that you practice adjusting the level of "firmness" of your recommendations (Telling) on how to do agile. I've found some coaches struggle to be assertive whereas others are over-assertive; balance is the key here. I rarely draw a line and do what I describe as a *hard* Tell; do it, not negotiable! But sometimes I do—usually when teams will cause problems for many other people through their behavior or they just do not have enough experience to make any decision on what the right answer is.

When is equally as important as the "how" as you "Tell." I find the best time to give advice is when it solves the problem at hand as it is happening. An even better opportunity to "Tell' is when the client has tried their idea/solution and it has not worked or has made the problem worse. Without adopting an "I told you so" attitude, you can then offer or even infer a different approach (your opportunity to Tell). Sometimes it is the coach's job to "let the train crash" by waiting for the client to fail with their idea before providing/Telling them your solution, but I'd use this strategy with extreme caution.

The best time to tell a client your opinion is, of course, after it has been requested, and sometimes this means you have to be patient as the client works through and experiences problems long enough to ask you for help. When they are ready to ask, you need to be there.

Tell: Practical Tips and an Experiment

Next time you see a clear, unambiguously "bad" idea being debated or discussed, practice assertive telling. Recently I was coaching a team that was conducting sprint planning before the sprint review. This is a great recent example where I used the Tell step.

The PM said to me, "Let's see what the team wants to do."

I said, "No, just move planning to after the sprint is finished; trying to plan work on the last day of a sprint makes no sense."

And do you know why they were doing this? Due to meeting room availability.

Other examples of when to Tell a team may include:

- "Do we really need to have a retro? Can't we skip it this sprint?"
- "I assigned this story to you. Is that OK?"
- The PO estimating how much development effort is required for a story.

It is important to be kind as you tell clients how to do agile and don't act like the agile police. Orient to serve/help your client, and adopt this mindset before telling; this helps your advice come across "softer." Play with how firmly you advise people; try offering your ideas to clients and only (very) occasionally insisting on a way to do agile. Pick the right moment to suggest and consider letting clients fail (just a little) before giving them the answer. But sometimes being assertive is best, so...

Try this experiment:

When you see an obviously sub-optimal practice or idea, be assertive and tell the individual or team what to do, instead of making a suggestion or offering advice.

Show

You may have heard of the phrase "show me, help me, let me." What this means is the agile coach initially *shows* the client how to do an agile practice, then partners with them, *helps* them do it, and finally *lets* the client perform the practice independently with the agile coach observing. The "Show" step of the Tell or

Show is meant to be used like this; as part of teaching the client how to do agile practices through the coach demonstrating them first.

I believe anyone delivering an agile coaching service must have, at some point, done what they are Telling or Showing others to do. This means that all agile coaches should have themselves been coached and shown how before they "Show" others. In other words, don't show a client how to do something until you've practiced doing it yourself with someone experienced. By working with a mentor, you will be able to get opportunities to be shown how to do agile ways of working (properly). Then, once you've become proficient at say, running a sprint review, you can show others how to do it.

Unfortunately, there are many people showing others how to do agile without ever having done it themselves—professional trainers who have little experience working with teams are one example. Always work with an experienced practitioner to learn how to do agile.

Showing clients how to do agile is usually part of a normal agile coaching approach. New agile teams often expect the person providing agile coaching to show them how to do practices and processes as they start their journey. So, don't be backward with new teams. Just step in and show them how to do agile; this will accelerate their adoption.

One tip is to ensure the team does not become reliant on you to do their agile for them. A sure sign this is happening is when the coach is not present and the team stops doing their agile practices, reverting back to old habits. A nice way to use the "Show" step is to periodically step in, show, then step back and observe the team, even let them fail or make mistakes for a few days/weeks. By letting the team try the agile practices after you've shown them, they can then utilize their retrospectives to inspect their own progress and suggest improvements.

Show: Practical Tips and an Experiment

Demonstrating how to do agile by stepping in and showing the team the answer is an important practice for an agile coach. This may come naturally to you, but some coaches find it difficult to step out in front of the team, take center stage, and Show everyone the answer. All scrum ceremonies, social contract creation, planning, and estimation together with practices like story mapping are opportunities to Show how agile works. A good agile coach has a well-developed Show capability.

I encourage you to actively seek out opportunities to observe your mentors doing the agile practices you're keen to learn;

once you have watched, then do them yourself prior to coaching others. Remember, though, do not allow your client to become reliant on you to do their agile for them. Show them once or twice, then have them try the practice themselves.

Try this experiment:

When you can see the team is struggling to understand what you're saying or suggesting, just show them or visually represent your idea, instead of verbally explaining what you mean.

Move 3: Open and Hold

If the across pathway and the "Tell or Show" move are the norm for typical agile coaching conversations, then the "Open and Hold" move and the down pathway can be considered the alternative or atypical. The "Open" step in this move of the model indicates an opening up of the conversation so it can go deeper than simply telling or showing clients what to do.

Coaches using this step of the model are able to talk with an open mind (put their opinions aside) and deal with their own emotions in order to make room for what the client thinks and feels.

Once the coach has opened up the conversation, they then "hold the space." Hold means not talking over the client, not giving opinions, and not judging what the client is sharing. By holding back your "stuff," it allows the client to express their thoughts and feelings without fear (of judgement). The coach holding back allows room for the client's thoughts, feelings, and opinions; this supports co-creation of the new, better way of working.

Open

The "Open" step refers to your ability to move a coaching conversation to dialogue (a discussion as opposed to a debate). This capability is usually one of the more difficult to develop due to the need to simultaneously unlearn old habits while you learn how to use the model outlined in this book.

Open refers to opening your mind and heart so that the client then does the same. If you, as the coach, can put aside your opinions and ask questions that provoke reflection and introspection in the client, you will be able to successfully execute this step.

To encourage yourself to have more "Open" conversations and be more open as a person, show vulnerability, let go of your preconceived answers, and show up to talk to others with this orientation. One suggestion is to have a short statement that helps you orient to this intent. At the start of your day, write it on a sticky note, place it on your desk and refer to it during all interactions throughout your day. It could read something like: *Today I will be curious about what others think before I offer what I think.*

These little reminder notes are useful and something I use all the time to support my orientation for the day as an agile coach—especially if I know I'm meeting with someone who has "triggered" me in the past.

The best way to improve your capability in opening the space is to practice with real conversations; these can be with clients or as a role play with your mentor. Once you start including these types of conversations into your life, you can track the percentage of "Open" versus "Tell" or "Show" steps you execute throughout a day.

The more you experiment with "Open and Hold" conversations, the more you'll see better coaching outcomes. Why? Because you now have the ability to respond to what the client needs instead of reacting with *your* answers/opinions. It creates a positive feedback loop; having a higher percentage of "Open and Hold" conversations is not only more fulfilling work for you but also provides better outcomes for the client and the organization. It's a win-win-win.

Open: Practical Tips and an Experiment

This step is closely related to your ability to respond (not react). In order to open a conversation, you need to be able to resist telling your client the answer. This is often easier said than done; hence, it is a practice.

Experiment with written notes to support you in orienting strongly towards being more open and curious with clients.

Here's a simple method to follow:

1. When you start a coaching conversation, pay attention to which move you take as you respond to the situation. Whether you choose "Tell or Show" or "Open and Hold" doesn't matter; just note which one.

2. Continue to do this daily and then, after a week, stop and review the percentage of conversations that are "Tell or Show" versus "Open and Hold."

3. Set yourself a percentage goal; maybe 50:50. Often coaches start out with almost 100 percent of their agile coaching conversations being "Tell or Show," but over time, this starts to shift towards more "Open and Hold" conversations.

4. In your journal reflect on how this exercise affects the quality of your work life and your coaching outcomes.

5. Work with your mentor/peers to discuss and improve your capability to respond with an "Open and Hold" conversation more often.

Try this experiment:

When you are facilitating a conversation where you choose to Open and Hold rather than Show or Tell, orient with compassion towards the other person, have an open mind and heart, and seek to understand by asking the individual, "What's on your mind?" then, genuinely, deeply listen, instead of showing up with a judgmental mind, a predetermined opinion, or a bias.

Hold

If you're opening the conversation and moving into a dialogue, then all you now need to do is hold this space by keeping your opinions out of it (the space). But this is more difficult than it sounds.

The "Hold" step represents one of the most difficult capabilities in the Responsive Agile Coaching model. "Holding the space" requires deep listening skills, high levels of self-awareness, and the self-discipline to maintain psychological safety for the client (not judging is key here). By self-discipline I mean not introducing your ideas or challenging the client's ideas when you aren't supposed to. If you are to hold the space, then you cannot be arguing with the client about whose idea is the best answer to the agile question being considered.

One of the best ways to build your capability to hold space is to experiment with silence and the pace of conversation. Recently, I facilitated a Meetup networking event where I live role-played an improvised coaching conversation in front of 45 agile coaches. It consisted of two role plays. In the first I used the Tell or Show move. The coaches wrote what they observed on Post-its and discussed the elements of the conversation. I then conducted a second role-play using the Open and Hold move. The coaches repeated their exercise of writing down what they observed.

The differences were stark, but the consistent observation was the use of silence, pauses, and the pace of the conversation. The way I conducted the second conversation seemed to be slower and more considered and respectful of the client, their experience, and needs.

Building your capability to Hold can be practiced all day; you don't need to be in an agile coaching conversation. Experiment with the pace of your responses to questions and use silence while you consider what a person just said; this pause changes the conversation because the other person can pick up on the fact that you're respecting the communication space and what the other person just put into it. Essentially, this capability is you getting control of your thoughts and behaviors by holding them back just a little bit longer than you normally would.

Hold: Practical Tips and an Experiment

Good agile coaches are knowledgeable, but great agile coaches know when to hold back this knowledge. In the Hold step, a responsive agile coach combines the self-discipline required to hold back knowledge with a non-judgmental approach while listening to the client they're coaching. This is the real secret of holding; to stop your internal "judger" from taking over your thinking or sneaking into the conversation as you coach.

During a conversation, slow down, do not automatically offer your ideas and opinion, practice this, and keep a journal of how successful you are at holding the space after you've opened it.

Role play with your mentor/peers and practice using silence during a conversation. I'll provide you with a more detailed question script in the "how to" section of this book (Part III).

Practice the "Hold" step in other parts of your life; often it's as simple as not talking (or forming your own opinion) for another second or two after the other person has finished what they were saying.

> *Try this experiment:*
>
> *When you are in a conversation with an individual or team, non-judgmentally listen to the other person and hold back your opinion, instead of quickly offering your advice.*

Move 4: Await Then Co-Create

If required, an agile coaching conversation can go deep into the *why* behind the *how* of agile. In this move the coach slows the conversation down, uses silence, and asks questions of the client that provoke introspection and reflection. In the Await step, the coach, after asking the right question, is quiet and waits for what emerges from the silence. What usually emerges are signs and signals that the client is ready and willing to start co-creating a better way of working with the coach.

This all sounds abstract and a bit "out there" right now, but trust me; it will all make more sense as I take you through the "How to Have a Conversation" in Part III of the book. For now though, let's go into this a little more by going through each step in this move.

Await

In order to build your capability to Await, you will need to be in coaching conversations that span sufficient time to allow you and the client to slow down and introspect on what is going on in the way of working. Even if you manage to get a few minutes with a client, you can use this as an opportunity to practice your Await step.

One simple way is to provide more time for clients to think when you ask them an open question like "What do you see as the way forward here?" While you are giving them time to answer, your job is to orient yourself by thinking, *I'm going to notice what's emerging*, then listen deeply to what the client says.

It is in these brief pauses that you're building your capability to pause and Await. This state of readiness is often when you see signs of the emerging opportunities (to work differently) that are coming as a result of the question you have just asked and the silence you provide.

A sure sign you are entering into the Await step is the client's answers to your questions start to come after longer and longer consideration; it is an indicator you are asking good questions as you Open and Hold the space. You have prompted the client to start introspecting.

I remember once I was coaching a leader of a health care company; a very quiet introvert who found it difficult to open up and talk in depth. I would be with this person for an hour-long coaching session and spend double my usual amount of time talking versus listening. But what was unusual about these sessions was the amount of time I spent in the Await step. I would ask a simple question like, "How did that feel when you had to face that emotional conversation?" Then I would spend the next minute or two in silence; I knew that this was how I could best serve this client, so I sat in readiness—open, supportive, and curious.

I had twelve sessions with this person as part of a larger coaching engagement, and my work with this client was what I perceived to be my most unproductive coaching engagement ever.

It was not until three years later I received an email from this person, now an executive. He had just moved into a new role as the CEO of a large institute. He wanted me to come in and work with his leadership team to help them grow and learn. He referred to the time we spent in those coaching conversations and the value he got from our work together.

The lesson I learned was that the value of the Await step is for the *client*; as a coach you may not see or experience this value. By Opening and Holding the space then Awaiting, you're serving the client, even if you don't always see the value.

AWAIT..... .

Await: Practical Tips and an Experiment

There's some magic that happens in a well-conducted coaching conversation, and it occurs here in the silence associated with the Await step. The client somehow makes a leap from where they were to a new, wider, more open world of options. It's amazing and takes me by surprise every time.

Unfortunately, I cannot explain the Await step completely; it is experiential and to be fully understood needs to be practiced. So, practice this step with a coach who has experience. Even if you don't think it is producing value as you practice, it is. Build your capability to wait for the future, use silence in combination with the right questions, then pay attention to what is emerging in the moment. The best way to monitor your development is, once again, to keep a journal of how and when you use this step and recording outcomes as well as your reflections when you do use Await.

Try this experiment:

When you are coaching a client, purposefully slow down the conversation, using extra pauses and silence, instead of filling silence with your ideas or opinion.

Co-create

It is amazing just how clients respond when they realize you're not telling them what to do but want to work with them to Co-create the solution together. I think this is so surprising for clients because it is uncommon for people to do this in the modern workplace. Everyone seems to want their idea or opinion recognized as the answer; people want to take credit for the solution and boost their standing in the organization. So, when a coach comes to them, offering to co-create the answer, it can take clients by surprise.

As an agile coach your job is to be authentic in your offer to co-create. If you do this, the client will respond accordingly and help create a way forward in the adoption of agile. If you are not genuine, then the client will likely intuit this, and the conversation could start to close down. Once the conversation starts to close down, the coach will no longer be holding the space, which makes co-creation impossible.

I recommend that you simply start asking the clients to work with you and be genuine in your offer. This is the best way to move the conversation towards action. There is an art to doing this. Ask the client to move forward to co-creation too early, and they feel pushed; if you do not ask early enough, the conversation stalls or goes nowhere. Remember, your job as a coach is to implement better ways to work, not just have nice, deep conversations. So, practicing the Co-create step is important for you to actually be an agent of change and not just a person who's good to have a chat with.

Co-creating is iterative and should start with small changes, experiments in what the way of working could become. Don't be afraid to simply brainstorm what the new way to work may look like with the client; no need to overcomplicate this step. Just remember, this step is preceded with the Open and Hold move, so make sure the space is opened first (I'll show you how to do this in Part III).

It's important to leave an agile coaching conversation with a small and safe first step to changing the way work is done where possible. Of course, it's OK if you don't always get to this point in a single conversation. Agile coaching often achieves its outcomes over a series of conversations, but experienced coaches can move a client from Open and Hold through to Co-creation in a 5- to 20-minute conversation. Sometimes that's not possible, and a coach must "circle back" a few times to close the conversation off and Embed a better way to work. I bring this up here because as you practice and build your capability, do not feel you always have to reach a point where the client agrees on a Co-created way forward. Aim to get to this point, but as you learn, don't be too disappointed if you don't manage to complete the entire Await then Co-create move all in one conversation.

Co-create: Practical Tips and an Experiment

If you've done all the preceding steps well, then co-creation seems to flow; but it is important to actually move to action and leave the conversation with a way forward. Practice the pace of moving the conversation towards co-creation; timing needs to be right, and you'll only learn by practicing. Just ask simple questions like: "Given what we've discussed, what can we do together to help improve how we work?"

As always, keeping a journal on your ability to move into and out of the Co-create step is a useful way to monitor your capability development.

Try this experiment:

When you are in a conversation, offer (not tell) your opinion into the co-creation process to come up with a shared answer, instead of pushing your idea as THE answer.

The End Point: Embed

All moves in the Responsive Agile Coaching model finish with a final step: Embed. Regardless of the preceding coaching activity, an agile coach should embed the change so that it "sticks." When the coach finishes working with a client, the best result is that the system of work keeps learning and improving on its own. That's the goal of Embed irrespective of whether the coach has utilized the across or down pathway.

Embed

The definition of the word embed says it all.

Fix an object firmly and deeply in surrounding mass.

The agile coach's job is to fix, firmly and deeply, the way of working into the surrounding wider business. The object is agile ways of working in the team/s; the surrounding mass is the wider organization. Or the object is an individual, and the surrounding mass is their place within an agile team.

81

It is beyond the scope of this book to undertake a review of organizational change management methods, but I do want to touch on some of what the research says about embedding change into an organization. Research that looked at implementing practice innovations inside hospitals concluded there are three key determinants to helping change stick:

1. Individual psychological: *helping individuals change their habits.*

2. Social: *holding teams accountable to agreed norms/behaviors.*

3. Structural processes: *implementing an agile framework and associated processes.*[4]

In the list above, I added the words in italics to indicate how we embed changes to the way of working (practice innovations) as agile coaches. I will outline more on each of the above points throughout the remainder of the book, but the point I'm making is that all three are required if you want to execute the Embed step correctly.

Checking that the way of working has "stuck" (is firmly fixed) is important. On a micro level with a single person, this is simple; keep checking in with the person and observe them under pressure to see if their behavior has changed. A sure sign the Embed step is done is what happens when the coach is not there. As a coach you need to set up feedback channels from other people who can give you real updates about whether the client's behavior is consistent with agile ways of working when you aren't around. These feedback channels allow you to know when your job is done and if the Embed step is complete.

But when you're coaching a larger system of work, it is more complex to complete the Embed step. Although practically this is one of the easiest steps for me to explain, it is one of the more difficult to ensure happens. An example of Embed done well is a team of agile teams I launched into new ways of working five years ago. I recruited and handed over my role as coach to another agile coach. I continued to mentor this person for six months, checking back in occasionally, even lending him support from time to time. This coach then passed on the role to another coach, who I also helped recruit, train, and mentor. We both supported this new coach over the next year. This agile team of teams is still running and improving their system of work and is a great example of the work required to embed changes to ways of working for a team of agile teams.

This is sometimes called "coaching back" once you leave an area of the business. My view is that if you have coached in an area, you never really leave it as long as you work in the organization. Keeping thin threads and contacts alive in that area and staying in touch with the coach or scrum master supporting the way of working should remain your responsibility, even if this is a simple phone call once every three months. This is not only a great way to Embed change but also keep your network and relationships healthy and strong.

Embed: Practical Tips and an Experiment

Get into the habit of coaching back and resist the urge to just walk away and forget when you formally finish coaching an area. Set up feedback channels for your clients so you can track if their behavior is embedded when you are not around to coach them.

Try this experiment:

After you have established a new practice, behavior, or ceremony with a team or individual, check back after two weeks to see if it has been embedded, instead of moving on to your next coaching engagement and forgetting your past work.

Chapter Summary

+ There are two pathways in the Responsive Agile Coaching model: across and down.

+ The responsive moment is a decision point where the agile coach chooses where to guide the conversation. Noticing this moment is an important first step to becoming more responsive.

+ The across pathway signifies a traditional agile coaching approach of telling or showing clients agile. The down pathway represents a less frequently used approach in agile coaching that involves opening and holding the space for deeper conversations.

+ Both pathways end with embedding the new way of working.

+ There are four "moves" and eight steps in the Responsive Agile Coaching model: Sense then Respond, Tell or Show, Open and Hold, and Await then Co-create.

+ The Responsive Agile Coaching model draws on concepts from Theory U and the Presencing Institute.

References and Further Reading

1. The idea for conversation pathways came from this book: Doug Silsbee, *Presence-Based Coaching*, (Jossey-Bass Publishing: 2008).

2. This book builds on the work from Otto Scharmer and the Presencing Institute: www.Presencing.org

3. Otto Scharmer, *Theory U: Leading from the Future as It Emerges*, (Berrett-Koehler: 2007).

4. Breckenridge JP, Gray N, Toma M, et al, "*Motivating Change*: a grounded theory of how to achieve large-scale, sustained change, co-created with improvement organisations across the UK," *BMJ Open Quality*, 2019.

5. Go to www.responsiveagile.coach to learn with others who have read or are reading this book; you can also visit www.responsiveagilecoaching.com for up-to-date content, downloads, and templates.

PART III
HOW TO DO RESPONSIVE AGILE COACHING

Introduction

In Part III, I want to walk you through how to actually have a responsive agile coaching conversation. I don't think I have ever seen anyone attempt to document how to execute agile coaching, let alone responsive agile coaching. I'm hoping to demystify the process and support beginners so that they can start coaching now—today. In the past, agile coaching has been reserved for expert, experienced agile practitioners. My intent with this part of the book is to "open source" agile coaching and make it something everyone can do, regardless of whether you are a change agent, leader, scrum master, project manager, or business analyst.

CHAPTER 6

HOW CONVERSATIONS WORK

Agile coaching conversations are usually based on a difference or gap. The client is seeking resolution to a problem or they have a question they need answered. Alternatively, the organization has a gap—the way people work now versus the desired, future way of working.

In agile coaching, questions are an important element that help to close or resolve the gaps between where we are and where we want to be with our way of working.

The focus of the rest of this chapter is learning how and when to ask which type of question. Before I provide you with a set of guiding questions, let's take a minute to understand the four levels of conversation that can take place during agile coaching. You need awareness of which type/level of conversation you are having at any moment with a client; this helps guide you on what questions to ask next during a conversation.

The Four Levels of Depth to Conversations

When your expert opinion or idea is not the right answer or when it is only a step toward discovering the right answer with the client, then the conversation needs to be deepened. The key to taking the conversation along to "down" pathway is asking the right types of questions and then listening in a different way.

The Presencing Institute has researched this area for over a decade and through their work they've identified how change agents, including agile coaches, can work with four different levels of conversation depth to bring change to people, teams, organizations, and society. Here's a summary for the four levels of depth.

1. **DOWNLOADING:** this type of conversation equates to traditional one-way training where knowledge is given to a recipient and they "learn" it. This is what happens in the "Tell or Show" move. Think of a child in school memoriz-

ing their multiplication tables. To use the metaphor of a computer, downloading means putting an app, or new data, onto an existing operating system. Agile coaches having conversations at this level provide knowledge or process guidance to clients without the client having to fundamentally change the way they operate (their mindset stays the same).

2. **DEBATE:** equates to individuals arguing their position or idea; this type of conversation would be best illustrated by an expert agile coach being unable to agree on the theoretical aspects of how to estimate a team's backlog when conversing with a product owner.

   If a coach attempts the "Tell or Show" move and is met with resistance, they will find themselves in a debate. Each person considers their opinion as fact and holds their ground on their position. Of course, a healthy difference of opinion is useful, but arguing about ways of working is risky; it is better to do the work and then talk about how to deliver value faster (with changes to way of working) than it is to have an abstract conversation on agile theory. Given the risk of an agile debate, I recommend that coaches conversing at this level quickly move the conversation down to level-3.

3. **DIALOGUE:** in a level-3 conversation, all participants reflect on the facts they see and how they feel about the situation. This level of conversation is required to execute the "Open and Hold" move. As a conversation moves into dialogue, each party starts to consider how

their actions play a part in the wider system of work. When in dialogue, each person moves from *being* their opinion to *having* an opinion. Think of a leader and an agile coach discussing the best way to implement a means to report on progress; each contributes to the conversation from their perspective so as to create a way forward that serves the needs of all. The task of the coach at this level is twofold:

+ To re-see the facts; consider their point of view in light of the bigger picture/system and be open to the other person's perspective (have an open MIND).

+ To help enable the client to have an open HEART; empathize with the other participant(s) in the conversation.

There are occasions where further depth is required in the conversation, where the client is seeking to understand the meaning or purpose of the changes being proposed to the way of working. This is when the fourth conversation level comes into play.

4. **COLLECTIVE CREATIVITY:** this level of conversation involves everyone having a moment of realization that enables the co-creation of new possibilities together; each person leaves the conversation different to when they entered. A level-4 conversation results in a shift in self and/or purpose for those in the conversation (open WILL). New insights have reframed each participant's perspective on the topic of conversation. The task for

the coach during this level of conversation is to "hold the space" for the client to feel fully heard and felt and provide their reflections. The coach holds the space by simply keeping their expertness out of the conversation; withholding telling while prompting with the right questions.

Flowing Through the Four Levels of Conversation

The diagram on the next page shows how an agile coach works through a conversation, moving across the four levels to achieve the coaching outcome of embedding a better way of working. Let me explain this flow and why and when the coach will take the conversation "down."

On an average day, agile coaches usually work with level-1 conversations; a client asks a question or requests help, and the coach responds with knowledge (tells) or shows the client how to do agile. The coach may then go on to Embed the learning by repeating this cycle until the client understands or is competent. This is our sunny-day scenario from earlier in the book.

But the conversation could move to level-2. Should the client resist the coach's advice, the conversation may move into a debate about what the "right" answer is.

When the client has an alternative opinion to what the coach suggests or the coach recognizes that a co-created way of working is the best option, then the "down" pathway is taken and the "Open and Hold" move is executed. When debate (level-2 conversation) happens, a capable agile coach will not try to win

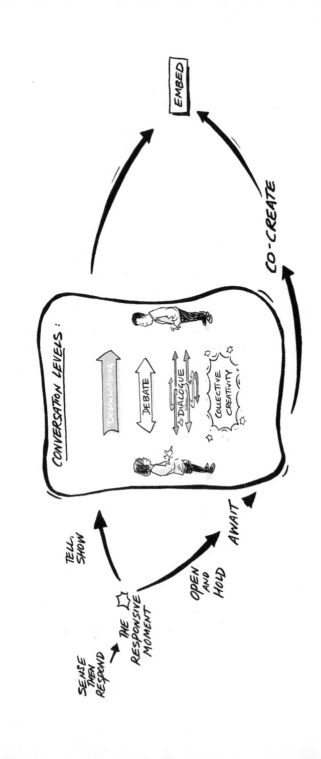

the argument but will work with the client to quickly move to a level-3 conversation (dialogue).

As the conversation moves "down" towards level-3, the coach is careful with their questions to ensure the client feels safe to offer a different view on the facts they see or explore their emotions in the conversation. Both the client and coach start to consider letting go of their opinions (the coach leads the way) and collectively they co-create a better way of working. Occasionally, the conversation needs to go deeper than mere dialogue; it's not just about the *way* we work or the process but *why* we work and *who* we are, that needs to be discussed. When this type of conversation is required, the coach moves with the client to a level-4 (collective creativity) conversation.

In a level-4 conversation, things can get personal for the participants in the conversation. Values, beliefs, long-held truths, and associated habits and behaviors are discussed. The agile coach helps the client consider these against the backdrop of moving to agile ways of working; the result is significant shifts in perspectives for those in the conversation. At level-4 there's a felt experience of change in the atmosphere of the conversation as a new sense of purpose or will is collectively discovered by participants. Not all conversations need to go here, but skilled coaches can move to this level when it serves the client to do so.

In the next chapter I'll go through each step in the Responsive Agile Coaching model with a guide on the types of questions required at each level of conversation.

Chapter Summary

- The Responsive Agile Coaching model describes the four levels of conversation a coach should be able to navigate.

- Downloading refers to giving clients information or new skills without the client having to change his/her mindset.

- Debate is when the client and the coach engage in an argument of ideas regarding agile ways of working. The coach seeks to move through this level to dialogue.

- Dialogue is an agile coach's natural conversation style that they always seek to come back to; it is where an exchange of ideas happens.

- Collective creativity is a deep conversation where new purpose or sense of self (role) is discovered through conversation.

CHAPTER 7.

MOVE 1: SENSE THEN RESPOND

This move begins prior to the start of the agile coaching conversation. Most of the activity in this move is happening in the internal world of the coach—in the mind, heart, and body—before they begin talking to the client.

In this chapter I'm going to outline what may appear to be a series of individual activities that happen in a specified order. However, please understand that these will not happen in a linear, sequential manner. In the Sense and Respond move, things can and will happen simultaneously or in a different order to how I present them here; that's OK. As you read, just consider the headings in this chapter as separate ideas that are interrelated under the one theme of sensing and responding.

Sensing: Scanning the System

Agile coaches should be scanning for signs or signals that indicate an opportunity to coach. This could be an observation of an individual's language or behavior, how a team is performing, or the flow of work through a larger system of work; these signs are the coach's "call to action."

Coaches usually sit to the side of a team; supporting, observing, and enabling change in the way work is done; this allows them to see the system from a distance because they are not inside it. Although at times it's useful for a coach to work in the team, especially at the start of a change to agile, the coach should try to maintain a distance and the ability to see the system. So my first piece of "how-to" advice to you is to create some distance from the team/s you're coaching.

From this perspective, the coach scans, waiting for an event or to be asked for help or for an opportunity to coach; it's then that the coaching conversation is "triggered."

The Trigger to Start a Coaching Conversation

Let's examine the triggers for an agile coaching conversation to commence. During the course of ongoing work, over and over again, I've noticed the same three triggers that signal to the agile coach that they are "on" and it is their time to step forward and play a role:

1. An **EVENT:** the coach is called upon by a specific event (planned or unplanned) involving the need to advise on ways of working. Examples include the launch of a new team or project/program of work.

2. An **ASK:** someone calls upon the coach to do, say, or show something related to ways of working. The best way to start a coaching conversation is when your services are requested (you obtain explicit permission to coach); we like this trigger.

3. An **OPPORTUNITY:** where the coach sees, perceives, or intuits that there's an opportunity to improve the way of working. This trigger can be frustrating to coaches, especially beginners, due to that fact that you do not have explicit permission to get involved but you see something in the way of working that is not optimized and believe there is value in doing something differently. The challenge here is getting into the conversation without appearing "pushy" or overly disruptive as you offer your idea/opinion. Great coaches do this well and know when the timing is right.

In mentoring many agile coaches, I have noticed that it is common for beginners to rely on triggers 1 and 2 and miss most of the triggers associated with type 3. This is especially prevalent with regards to working with more senior people in the organization. Beginner agile coaches hear a "leader" ask for something and quickly react, doing whatever it is without questioning the intent; they miss the opportunity to affect change in the leader's behavior. Beginner agile coaches' sensing abilities have also yet to be developed, so they do not see the opportunities as an experienced coach would, or they see the opportunities but are not confident to step up and into a conversation. We'll discuss how to develop this capability later.

When the coach is triggered into action, they are *affected*, which can result in automatic reactions from the coach—usually at the expense of the client's needs. Let's quickly stop and consider how you can manage your "self" when triggered into action.

You Are Affected

When a trigger signals the start of a coaching conversation (or the potential to conduct one), you are *affected*. In other words, you are *influenced or touched by an external factor* as you sense your environment.

Common ways in which you are affected when triggered into action as an agile coach include:

- You start telling yourself stories to help explain the situation.

- You have a physical reaction in your body; you tense up, or your blood pressure rises.

- You feel emotions, such as frustration, curiosity, compassion, or excitement.

- You have ideas, opinion, thoughts, or solutions or come up with options for what to do.

- Your intuition sends you signals or sensations.

The challenge for coaches is to notice any or all of these and ensure they do not result in unhelpful, reactive behavior. The coach aims to maintain an orientation focused on serving the client; they resist letting their emotions or ideas come into the conversation in a manner that is not productive. In other words, the agile coach must consciously respond and not habitually react to the trigger and any associated affects.

Once an "opportunity to coach" moment arrives, your reaction or response will significantly impact the quality of the coaching conversation that will follow. It is in this moment that your personality and associated traits want to take a shortcut to getting the outcome (follow a habit). Your normal reaction that you've learned and been rewarded for over your lifetime ensures your previously utilized, routine habits are engaged to produce what you believe to be a predictable outcome; you get your reward. I'll unpack how habits work later; for now, just realize that these automatic routines may not always serve your client.

One great thing about agile coaching is that the role requires new habits that sometimes run against the coach's regular routines; in short, agile coaching done right requires the coach to grow and develop. This is typical in any field in the sense that the habits that helped you at the start of your career often do not serve you as your career matures. The new habit a responsive agile coach requires is to act differently in the moment of choice; I call this the responsive moment. If you're not paying attention, you could miss it; fortunately, I have some ideas for you on how to ensure you notice this important moment.

Your First Action: STOP

If you are a responsive agile coach, your immediate action when you are triggered into a coaching conversation is to pause (do nothing), even if this is just for a moment. In this pause you create a gap or space between the trigger and what happens next. By creating this gap, you maintain your ability to be responsive and avoid falling into reactive, habitual routines. Here's a suggested sequence: you stop, observe, consider, observe some more, and then question the question.

COACHING CONVERSATION

This questioning of the question is a sneaky way to enlarge your gap even more while you work out the best response. I suggest you "question the question" firstly in your own mind and then with the client if appropriate. I'll give you some example questions in a minute, but for now, just remember to stop and observe as your first response.

Orient Your Intent to Serve

Just before an agile coach responds, possibly during the responsive moment or before, they should orient themselves in readiness for the coaching conversation. It is important to ensure you have the right mindset. I have one universal orientation I recommend to agile coaches.

Orienting yourself to "serve the client AND the organization" sounds simple enough, but it is a critical aspect of responsive agile coaching. I'll explain the science behind this in following sections, where I take you through an actual conversation, but setting your intent before the conversation starts is a preemptive step that prepares the scene (and your mindset).

Here's what I mean by orienting; let's start with what the dictionary says: *"Align or position (something) relative to the points of a compass or other specified positions."*

An agile coach's compass should be set to serving the client while staying true to the organization.

The organization's objectives together with the client's needs form the compass bearing for the agile coach to which they align. Check in with yourself that you are showing up with the right intent and in service of the client; there's nothing *self*-serving about agile coaching. How do I get my orientation right? I maintain my mindset as a coach by always asking myself a core question prior to entering into a conversation.

Agile Coaching's Core Question

Agile coaches always have the same core question that defines the reason their role exists, and it is an overarching tool to focus the conversations they have with clients. Agile coaching differs from professional coaching (life or leadership coaching) because we have this core question behind all our work. Professional coaching conversations have an agenda that is 100 percent driven by what the client wants to discuss; the opening question to start a professional coaching conversation is usually something like: *"What's on your mind?"* or *"What would you like to talk about today?"*

Agile coaching, however, has a consistent, underlying core question. It's always the same question or a variation of this question: *"How can I help, serve, and support you to adopt agile ways of working?"*

This is our topic. We can talk about lots of related topics like culture, empowerment, roles and responsibilities, or theories, but at the end of the day, we're here to help people learn about, do, and ultimately be agile. This may involve personal transformation or a simple process implementation, but regardless, the core question is the same and serves as a compass that the agile coach uses to maintain alignment as they work.

So, with this underlying question as the reason a client would talk to an agile coach as a given, we then need to understand how a typical conversation can progress along one of the previously mentioned pathways.

We've set our orientation to align with what the client wants and what the organization needs; now we can actually start a coaching conversation. No, not yet; you need to get permission to do that.

Permission to Coach

Pushing your thoughts, ideas, opinions, or enquiries onto someone is not always appropriate and can come across as intrusive or plain rude. One critical aspect of agile coaching is that you need to be invited to coach by clients. The way you get invited is by asking permission to coach. If you don't get permission, you can't coach. If you don't have permission, you can still observe and sense the environment until either asked to help or another opportunity to serve presents itself.

Getting permission does not have to be complicated. I use a simple approach that limits what you're asking of the client.

Key question: "Have you got five minutes?"

As you ask for permission, keep sensing, listening, and observing. The client will be sending you signals, body language, and other clues that provide you with information as to their readiness to enter into a coaching conversation. Watch for curious facial expressions as opposed to crossed arms or defensiveness.

Sometimes you will be asked to coach a team that has not given you permission. This is quite normal; in this situation, your permission has been given to you by your sponsor to implement new ways to work with the team; your job is to build rapport, trust, and commitment in the team (i.e. coach them).

Question the Question

Questioning the client's question is part of sensing because you are not coaching yet; you are still checking to see what your response is going to be. When an agile coach is asked to provide advice or show a client how to do agile, it's important to question the question. This can be done in a respectful way so as to understand the problem being solved before proposing a solution. This approach is important due to the high prevalence of clients asking coaches to do something that sounds like a good idea, but the coach knows from experience that it is not; the coach has been down that path before and knows where it leads. Solving the client's problem can only be done if the coach knows the intent behind what the client is attempting to do. Here's a great question to have ready if you are unsure of the problem you're being asked to solve:

Key question: "What are we trying to achieve here?"

Once you're clear and are confident you're about to help solve the right problem, you can then respond accordingly; you can make a move to serve the client either through "Tell or Show" or "Open and Hold." You have arrived at the responsive moment.

The Responsive Moment – React or Respond

When we consider the Responsive Agile Coaching model, there are three response options available to the agile coach when they arrive at the responsive moment:

1. Say and do nothing; keep sensing (listen, observe).

2. Offer some advice or do something to help or demonstrate (Show or Tell move).

3. Ask an open question, listen; hold back your opinion/judgement (Open and Hold move).

When I mentor agile coaches, I'm always looking to expand or enlarge the responsive moment. As previously mentioned, you can consider this moment to be a gap between the coach being affected and their reaction or response. The larger the gap, the more opportunity the coach has to choose how to respond. All of the preceding content of this chapter aims to help you make the most of this moment when it arrives.

The obvious next question is: "How do I know which pathway to choose?" The answer is a combination of what the client needs, what the circumstance allows the coach to do, and what the client is ready for. I'll provide some specific guidance on this in later parts of the book, but I do have some general advice. Rather than providing you with an extensive set of criteria to use when choosing, I recommend an agile approach. If you have the prerequisites for a sunny-day coaching scenario (sponsorship, clear problem and the right skills/experience) then proceed to Tell or Show your client—because that's what they're expecting you to do. If you are unsure if the sunny-day prerequisites are in place, then I recommend you start with what you think, feel, and/or intuit is the right pathway by saying or asking something, then keep sensing what happens next. If your client needs some quick information and you have the knowledge and the situation is right, then just Tell or Show them what they need. If your answer is met with resistance, try an Open and Hold move (I'll show you how later), then keep sensing and Await. The pathway will present itself and, as long as you keep sensing as you converse with the client, you can pivot as required.

Before we get onto the other moves, I'd like to run through an example conversation that demonstrates the Sense then Respond move.

A Sense Then Respond Conversation

Here's an example of the Sense then Respond move in a conversation flow.

John is an agile coach for a team; after the morning team stand-up, he observed Mary talking with another team member about the upcoming retrospective.

"I have to send out the invites for our next retrospective; this time I'm not inviting Fred. Not after what happened last time," Mary said.

Upon hearing this, John felt his face flush with frustration. Fred was the product owner of the team, and this was the third time Mary had excluded him from the retrospective—despite John previously advising against it. John was about to jump into the conversation when he caught himself being emotionally reactive. Instead, he took a deep breath, calmed himself, and spoke the silent mantra that he used whenever he was about to enter into an agile coaching conversation: "John, you're here to help and serve both the organization and your client."

"Have you got a minute, Mary?" John said.

"Sure, what's up?" Mary responded.

"I noticed you're going to exclude John from the retrospective next week. What are we trying to achieve? What's our intent here?"

Mary quickly shot back somewhat defensively: "To have a safe space for the team to talk and discuss how to improve. With Fred attending, it's not safe; he talks over everyone"

"Wow, OK, I didn't know that Fred was causing such problems; what can I do to help?" John replied.

Let's debrief on this example.

Realizing this is an agile coaching "moment," John (the coach) acknowledged how he was affected when he was called into action. He then paused to provide himself time to respond. John then oriented his mindset to serve Mary as best he could, considered Mary's need, asked permission to coach, and then *responded* with a question that questioned the intent of what Mary was about to do.

Instead of jumping to execute a reactive Tell or Show move (telling Mary to invite Fred to the retro), John questioned the question—after checking his own orientation. Then, after he had obtained the context of the situation, John was better able to respond.

Chapter Summary

◆ "Sense" happens before the agile coaching conversation starts and involves the agile coach scanning for opportunities to coach. A keen sense of awareness is required to ensure the coach does not miss the signals that they are "on" and it's their time to do their job.

◆ An agile coach's first action is to STOP, observe, and consider their options.

◆ Checking your intent and seeking permission to coach are both prerequisites for an agile coaching conversation.

CHAPTER 8.

MOVE 2: TELL OR SHOW

After the responsive moment, we can follow one of two pathways: across or down. Let's first look at the across pathway: a conversation where the coach's move is to Tell or Show the client the what or how of agile.

Caution: Downloading Risks Repeating Old Patterns

The risk when a coach gives advice without pausing to consider their response, is that the client will take the advice and adjust the information to fit into or on top of their old mindset. We compared this in the previous chapter to downloading an app into an old operating system. We have a saying as agile coaches: *"Downloading is like putting old wine into new bottles."*

So, the word of caution here is for the coach to double check the intent of the client's question (question the question). Often there is a deeper conversation, an "Open and Hold" conversation, just below the surface if only the coach would ask the right question.

Of course, nothing is as infuriating as a coach answering every question with a question; a lot of the time it's appropriate for the agile coach to act as a subject matter expert and provide answers to questions. In these situations, Tell or Show is the right move to take. Let's discuss how.

Tell Them; Show Them

If you sense the client is accepting of your ideas or advice and a deeper conversation is not required, then proceed to help them learn in the traditional manner. Instruct (Tell) them and/or Show them how to do agile. You can then follow up by repeating these cycles or learning loops, finishing the coaching engagement by checking the agile practice has been adopted and embedded into how people are working. This is the typical sunny-day scenario where the coach's ideas and advice are either the right answer or the best place to start and the client is not resisting the change.

When utilizing the Tell or Show move of the model, the coach should consider how the client processes information and learns. The end result for the adoption of agile as a way to work is for the client to have observable behavior change. Many arguments have been had regarding how much instruction is required before a learner should simply learn by doing. My usual pattern is as follows: "Tell them, show them, let them".

In this learning process the coach instructs the client on how to do an agile practice or process, then, possibly at a later time, demonstrates how to do the practice, and finally, the coach lets the client do the new practice while they observe. To ensure the practice is becoming the new normal, the coach periodically returns to assess how the client is working and may provide further advice and guidance. This cycle is repeated until the practiced behavior is embedded as a normal way to work for the client.

Coaches need to develop their skills in explaining concepts clearly, checking for comprehension and that the client has understood the information the coach is imparting.

It is beyond the scope of this book to go deeply into learning theories, and many better reference books have already been written on these topics. What the agile coach needs to understand is that instructing, teaching, and assessing the client's competence is an important part of a coach's role, and so learning how to teach clients should be in every coach's development plan. I want to now take you through how an actual agile coaching conversation flows when this move is used.

Let's continue the conversation between John and Mary regarding Fred's behavior at retro. Here's how to initiate an agile coaching conversation by asking for permission.

"Have you got a minute, Mary?" John said.

"Sure, what's up?" Mary responded.

"I noticed you're going to exclude John from the retrospective next week. What are we trying to achieve? What's our intent here?"

Mary quickly shot back somewhat defensively: "To have a safe space for the team to talk and discuss how to improve. With Fred attending, it's not safe; he talks over everyone"

"Wow, OK, I didn't know that Fred was causing such problems; what can I do to help?" John replied.

Mary: "Well, I'm happy for you to help, but as we've discussed many times, psychological safety is a very important aspect of high-performing teams, and Fred often shouts over everyone and pushes his opinion onto the team. This shuts everyone down, and the retro is not effective, as everyone is nervous about Fred's loud voice."

John: "What's the intent of a retro, Mary? Who does it serve?"

Mary: "It helps the team improve how they work together."

John: "And who's in the team?"

Mary: "Yeah, OK, I hear you. Fred is in the team; I get where you're going."

John: "How about I come and support the retro and work with Fred on his behavior before and during the retro?"

Mary: "As long as he doesn't derail another retro like he did last month. Thanks, John; if you could co-facilitate the retro, that would be great."

John: "Can do."

Mary: "Thanks, John. Good compromise; I'll let everyone know."

John has done his job by utilizing the Tell or Show move; specifically, just the Tell aspect of it.

Another example would be the agile coach demonstrating how to do an agile practice while the team or individuals observe. This is most common during the launch of new agile teams; at this time, the team has low levels of knowledge and skill, so showing them what to do is both helpful and appropriate.

But what would happen if John's coaching suggestions are not as well received by Mary? What if when John asks for permission to coach, the answer to the question is "no"? Simple; then John does not have permission to coach. That's the end of this interaction (for now).

Of course, even if you do get permission to start a coaching conversation, your suggestions may not be welcomed; your insights/suggestions may be disregarded when offered during the conversation. When this happens, the coach and client are in a *debate* type (level-2) conversation. If this happens, the agile coach should explore taking the conversation deeper using the Open and Hold move.

Chapter Summary

- The Tell or Show is the most common move made by agile coaches; unfortunately, it is usually a reaction and not a response to a situation.

- The Tell or Show move is aligned to instructing or teaching services; however, it is still an important element of the overall Responsive Agile Coaching model.

CHAPTER 9.

MOVE 3: OPEN AND HOLD

The alternative down pathway for an agile coaching conversation is when the coach's ideas or advice are not the best solution for the situation, or the coach is met with resistance from the client. The coach needs to put aside their opinions to enable a dialogue with the client.

In an effort to quickly move on from debate to dialogue, the coach needs to responsively change their approach if the Tell or Show move is not working during a client conversation. If this happens, the coach moves the conversation "down" by asking different questions—very specific types of questions. The coach stops advising and "telling" and opens their mind by putting aside their opinions. This is what responsiveness is—pivoting your approach mid-conversation to accommodate the client.

As we start on the down pathway, I want to take a minute to explain what's going to happen during the Open and Hold move. The diagram below shows the map of how conversations can

flow down through the open MIND, open HEART, and open WILL. In the following sections I'm going to guide you through the down pathway utilizing the Open and Hold move. I want to highlight that not all conversations have to go all the way to level-4; often a dialogue (level-3 conversation) is enough to start working with the client and move the conversation towards co-creating and embedding the change.

I'll start with open MIND questions first and then follow the pathway down from there, showing you the type of questions to use at each level.

Questions to Enable an Open MIND

Open MIND questions aim to take the conversation from a debate (level-2) down to a dialogue (level-3). The coach puts aside their expert knowledge of agile and opens their mind (and other senses) to what the client is saying and doing.

Here is an important tip when asking open MIND questions; you cannot help a client to open their mind unless you first open yours. It is a common mistake of agile coaches to carry a closed and opinionated mindset into a coaching conversation and pretend (or think) they have an open mind. In this situation the agile coach is really still holding onto their ideas and opinions and waiting for the moment to "convince" the client they (the expert) are right and their answer is the way forward. In case you think you can trick clients into opening their minds, I'm going to let you in on a little-known secret: *Clients know your truth; they intuit your mindset.*

OK, that's a big claim, but it's founded in research. Recent studies show that science's best hypothesis about how intuition works is that the brain records and is noticing inputs from the senses and is filing them away for reference. When your brain wants a shortcut to an answer, especially when there's no time to think it through, parts of the brain make decisions based on a limited number of these filed inputs. Let's take a minute and look at the neuroscience behind intuition.

The Neuroscience of Intuition

Neuroscience is any or all of the sciences which deal with the structure or function of the nervous system and brain. A lot of what we do as coaches can be explained by this area of science. I suggest you do more reading on this subject; it's not only fascinating but will help you as a coach.

I wanted to take a moment to bring science into the conversation because I know there are a lot of people out there who need a bit of research on a topic before they take a concept seriously (people like me). I want to reinforce the link between the agile coach being genuine and their ability to take a coaching conversation down from levels 1 and 2 to levels 3 and 4. To illustrate my point, I want to, for a moment, use a non-agile example to explain how neuroscience views intuition; I'll then relate it back to agile coaching conversations.

Imagine you're driving a car in busy traffic and a noisy, beat-up truck that's blowing dirty exhaust comes up next to you. The angry driver takes his cigarette out of his mouth and starts yelling at you to get out of his way. Apparently, he thinks you cut him off when you changed lanes. You are stressed and under pressure when the traffic stops, and it looks like the truck driver is going to get out of his vehicle. Without thinking, you act to lock the car door, check that your phone is nearby, and tense your body while mentally running through the self-defense stances you were taught eight years ago. All of this happens in 0.47 of a second, but you are ready for whatever happens next.

This example is similar to the one used in a recent and important research paper on the neuroscience of intuition, published in the *Brain and Cognition Journal*. In this paper S.J. Segalowitz explains what is happening in the brain in such situations:

> *"Anticipating the movement of other vehicles on the road also involves judging the road conditions, the state of the traffic signals ahead, as well as the other drivers' intentions based on their interpretations of these factors and their internal states. Many of these judgments are based not only on visual, but also on auditory, proprioceptive, and even olfactory and social cues."*

The authors conclusion is that the brain cannot possibly compute its way through the world but predicts what will happen by using past sensory "data" from a lifetime of experience. In any given moment, the brain is efficiently guessing or predicting what will happen next, then reconciling this afterward with any follow-up data; it's called pre-cognition. The authors put it like this:

> *"The brain continuously employs memory of past experiences to interpret sensory information and predict the immediately relevant future...a fundamental function of the brain is to predict proximate events, which facilitates interactions with external stimuli, conserves effort, and ultimately increases the chances of survival."* [1]

So, what does this have to do with a coaching conversation? Well, during an agile coaching conversation, your client's brain is checking almost constantly (about six times per second) for threats, making sure they are safe from harm, and maintaining their chances of survival. Your client's brain is using its entire lifetime of experience to check to see if you are genuinely there to help; it's checking constantly, then predicting what's going to happen next, poised to "shut down" the depth of conversation if it is perceived as potentially harmful. Of course, we're not talking about physical harm but psychological; this is exactly what people refer to when they talk about psychological safety.

Coaching conversations that go down to levels 3 and 4 involve the client being vulnerable; opening up to being judged (for their opinion) or shamed (for showing emotion). The client's brain is like a spring-loaded trap waiting to snap shut at any sign of (psychological) danger coming from a coach. If you are not 100 percent genuinely open and there to serve your client, their brain will intuitively know and start to predict using all of the client's sensory inputs—sight, sound, smell, and all the data from all social interactions they've ever had. If you are not mindful of what you say and do and have not properly oriented yourself prior to the conversation, then you do not stand a chance of "tricking" your client (and their brain) that you are genuine. David Rock, a renowned researcher in the neuroscience of leadership, puts it this way:

> *"...in a threatened state, people are much more likely to be 'mindless.' Their attention is diverted by the threat, and they cannot easily move to self-discovery."* [2]

If you're coaching someone and your mindset has not been set (oriented) to serving the client, then it doesn't matter what you say; the client will sense you are not genuinely open and therefore will not open up their own mind. You'll be stuck in debate mode. The client's brain will accurately predict you are not a "safe" person to be opening up to and will remain closed. We're starting to get into territory here that involves you, the coach, closely paying attention to your inner state as you ask questions. Assuming you have your inner state under control and have oriented yourself to serve your client, here are four open MIND questions to try:

Key question: "I'm sensing this is not quite right for you; what's on your mind?"

Or any of these:

> "Hey, just checking in with you; what are your thoughts on the change to agile?"

> "What's on your mind?"

> "I'm just here to serve you in the best way I can and have no agenda; what do you think is going on here?"

The intent of these types of questions is not to evoke any emotional response from the client but to enquire about how they see the facts. Open MIND questions are not asking the client to be emotionally vulnerable but seek the client's opinion on what they are seeing is going on. Often these types of questions are enough to move to co-creation with the client and progress the coaching conversation forward.

Remember that the above question must be asked with the agile coach having an open mind. The coach must be genuine and not have an agenda or try to trick or manipulate the client into agreeing with them. Any attempt by the coach to coerce the client to agree with their opinion will most likely result in the client's intuition shutting down the dialogue (level-3) and will move the conversation back to a debate (level-2).

Sometimes the agile coach will sense that the client wants or needs to open their heart and discuss how they feel about the situation. It is this level of conversation that I see as the biggest gap in the senior agile coach market. Having heartfelt conversations does not mean you are a psychologist or counselor; it simply recognizes that changing to an agile way of working can involve human emotions. The next set of questions shows you how to work with an open HEART, but before we go there, I need to discuss the other element of the "Open and Hold" move. "Holding the space" is essential, so I want to ensure we're aligned on exactly what it means for agile coaching.

How to HOLD the Space

An important aspect of the down pathway in the Responsive Agile Coaching model is the ability to hold. What is the coach holding exactly? Well, let me explain with a metaphor story. Imagine a scene with two people communicating; now between them, visualize a space with a perfectly prepared six-foot-wide, one-foot-high, circular garden bed filled with pure white sand that has been leveled smooth. The coach and the client in this activity will be communicating initially without talking. Both participants are sitting on cushions at the edge of the circular sandpit, each holding a thin metal stick.

A conversation starts between the two people sitting at the edge of this circular sandpit. Now think of each person's contribution to the conversation as them carefully drawing with their stick what they intend to communicate to the other into the perfectly level sand.

The ideal communication process is for one person to complete the full drawing in the sand that represents their contribution, then allow time for people to look at this and attempt to make sense of it. If this was a group of people, everyone would have a few minutes to take in the contribution, and each person could ask clarifying questions on what they see/interpret. Ideally there would be time for the space to be reset, the sand leveled off before another person contributes their idea into the conversation.

This process of allowing people to fully articulate their ideas into the conversation space and then asking clarifying questions is the best way I've found to allow for the encoding and subsequent decoding of messages into and out of a communication space between people. By encoding I mean the message a person is trying to get across through their contribution to a conversation. Unlike the sandpit example, agile coaching has messages encoded into words, gestures, and body language during the conversation. The person listening has the job of decoding the message from the contributor—getting the meaning from what has been encoded. Good communication simply means the intended message that is encoded into a conversation space is decoded without the message getting lost in translation.

Now let's contrast the above process with what normally happens in workplace conversations. Multiple people have their sticks in the sand at the same time, hardly letting others finish their drawing before they scribble over it with what they believe is a better idea or contribution. Nobody is respecting or holding the space for an individual to communicate their full idea. People are too invested in their own idea to take the time to understand what the others are attempting to communicate. Questions are mostly interrogative and are not open; rather than clarifying, they simply start a debate of ideas. No one even tries to fully decode the other participants' contributions.

"Holding the space" during an agile coaching conversation simply means letting the client complete their contribution and asking clarifying questions to fully understand what they are attempting to communicate. When the client is in the process of opening up and being vulnerable, a poorly phrased or ill-timed question can disrupt the psychological safety at any moment; shutting the conversation down and reducing or stopping the ability for the client to consider changing the way they work.

Here's an experiment I suggest you run. Next time you ask a question or are in a conversation with others, watch for moments when there is an awkward silence. During this silence, observe yourself and notice what "urges" come up in your head (self-talk). What is dying to come out of you and into the space? This is your "stuff," and it needs to be checked prior to being put into the space to ensure it serves the client.

I'm hoping you now see the importance of an agile coach's ability to "hold the space" for a client. The "space" that I'm referring to is the atmosphere of the conversation, sometimes called the relational field. When two or more people are together, a field is generated. The concept of "space" or "atmosphere" is more obvious at sporting events or music concerts, but it is present in coaching conversations and business meetings too. I'm sure you've been in meetings where the feeling "in the air" was light and creative and other times when it was tense and heavy or combative. This is the space we work in and with as agile coaches.

The questions I took you through in the previous sections of this chapter are the means to generate the right atmosphere, but it is by listening that you hold the space for the client. Listening, together with following my "Things NOT to Do as You Hold the Space" list in the next section, will give you the best chance at holding the space for your conversation as the client moves towards the Co-create step and a new way forward with you.

Things NOT to Do as You Hold the Space

I have to pause us here to make a few points on what NOT to do as you execute the Open and Hold move, taking the conversation down to levels 3 and 4; from debate to dialogue. Here's a list of do not dos; things that will disrupt the space or the coach-client connection:

- **Don't ask "Why?":** "Why" questions challenge the client's opinions, ideas, or even their beliefs and truths. You will risk the client intuiting the possibility that the conversation is not psychologically safe. It shuts the dialogue down instead of enabling an open MIND/HEART.

- **Don't offer advice:** You might think you're helping, but you're not, so don't give advice. This is your expertness trying to sneak back into the conversation. Suspend this mindset and stay in service of the client. If you put your opinion into the conversation, it could say to the client's intuition that their ideas are being judged, and they may revert back into debate—your opinion against theirs. Usually coaches guess that their advice will help, only to find it does the opposite, stifling the client's ability to be creative.

- **Don't ask questions that are actually suggestions:** This is a variation of "Don't offer advice." Simply offering a solution and putting a question mark at the end doesn't mean it is really a genuine open question. It is, again, the agile expert trying to get back into the conversation. If you are taking over with your ideas, stop it! This will move the conversation back to debate and away from a dialogue.

- **Don't judge:** It is easy to use tone and/or language that signals you are judging what the client is saying. Once I had a coach who I was mentoring who would always affirm that he agreed with me when we were in a coaching conversation. "Yes, agreed," he would say, as if this was helping me feel safe. It wasn't. I felt judged and was defensive. This meant his mindset carried opinion and was judgmental; he was assessing the quality of what I was saying. Similarly, a coach I previously mentored would comment that the client's contribution to the conversation was "beautiful"; this evaluation was also judgmental and not helpful.

- **Don't indulge yourself:** Sometimes you have been through a similar experience to the client and want to share stories or indulge in the conversation topic; to gossip or be self-righteous with them. Don't do this; it's serving you, not the client.

Without the ability to hold the space, a coach cannot move the conversation to a deeper, emotional level, which is why this section is a prerequisite for what follows. Having open HEART conversations requires high levels of psychological safety, and for this the coach must have at least basic proficiency in holding the space.

Questions to Enable an Open HEART

The short description behind the intent of open HEART questions could be "conscious kindness." As a coach you are paying close attention to your intent and orienting yourself towards being kind as you converse with the client. Through attempting to understand the client's position and feelings on how they are experiencing the change to ways of working, you enter into open HEART conversations. This works in one-on-one settings or with the whole team as a check-in.

The ability to take a conversation down into this territory is, in my opinion, a critical prerequisite to becoming a responsive agile coach. Working with emotion is a key differentiator of the best agile coaches. Why? Well, because people's behavior is strongly determined by emotion. Consider this quote from an article in *Psychology Today* titled "Like it Or Not, Emotions Will Drive the Decisions You Make Today" by Mary C. Lamia Ph. D.

> *"If your brain comes across something it appraises as a 'red flag,' you'll be sent a general, vague alert in the form of the feelings and thoughts that are created by an emotion. This somewhat imprecise signal alerts you to pay attention. In this way, your emotions serve as a cueing system—an attention directing system associated with physiological changes that can prepare you to take action."* [3]

During a conversation, an agile coach can tap into how a client is feeling about a particular situation as a means of moving the conversation to a dialogue and away from a debate. Often by simply asking how a client is feeling the coach can move the conversation along towards co-creating a way forward. The agile coach is fully appreciating the client's situation, genuinely cares for them, and orients towards serving them in their role as a coach. If done correctly, the client knows that the coach feels the emotions they're going through; I call this sensation the client "feeling felt." The generic term is empathy. So, what are the questions required here? Well, they're quite simple but powerful. If you can let a client verbalize their emotions, it can take a lot of the "heat" out of an argument, rapidly build rapport, and take the conversation out of debate. Here are some questions to practice.

Key question: "How are you?"

Now what's important here is that the client, like most people, is conditioned to respond with an impersonal answer; something like "We're doing OK. I'm fine. No problems."

The coaching challenge is to get a genuine answer from the client and an answer that is first-person; using "I" instead of "we." If the client starts talking about how the team feels, the coach must redirect the conversation to the first-person (how the client feels); otherwise, you are talking about things outside of the client's control; you're now problem solving a team issue and no longer in a one-on-one coaching conversation. Of course, team-based mood "pulse-checks" are good too, but if you're coaching one-on-one, just be on the lookout for your client avoiding talking about *their* feelings. Clients do this to deflect from having to discuss their inner world of emotions, but responsive coaches can take them there gently and carefully for their benefit.

Where I live in Australia, it is culturally inappropriate to discuss feelings, especially in the workplace. This has resulted in many charities being established to deal with the resulting mental health problems this causes. One of the charities that's attempting to help solve this problem has a mission that is useful for us when considering agile coaching conversations. RUOK. org.au aims to reduce suicide; one of its missions is to *"inspire and empower everyone to meaningfully connect with people around them and support anyone struggling with life."* [4]

What I like about their approach is its simplicity; simply ask a question, such as "Are you okay?" Then, genuinely listen to the answer. I usually add one follow-up question when the person I ask gives a typical Australian answer, such as, "Yeah, no worries. I'm fine." I ask this follow-up question as I look them in the eye and give them my full attention:

"No, really, <<insert their name here>>, how are you?"

There are many variations of this question; I've listed some below, but I encourage you to find one that you feel comfortable asking and then practice.

"How are you feeling about the change to agile?"

"How are you feeling?"

"How are you doing today?"

Remember, the key is to ask while you carry an open mind and heart (conscious kindness); otherwise, the client's intuition will detect you're not being genuine and start to shut down the conversation.

Questions to Enable an Open WILL

Some agile coaches I've been mentoring recently have brought up the topic of purpose of work or meaningful work. A lot of my coaching is in helping coaches and others align their work lives with their purposes and internal motivations. In fact, I recently surveyed 37 agile coaches, who I provided mentoring and development for over a six-month period; I asked them, "What drew you to want to become an agile coach?" 79% responded with "To make a difference" or "To have more meaning in my work."

My point is that coaches find it adds meaning to their work to make a difference in the lives of those they are coaching. This is a consistent theme for other coaches I've worked with and, of course, is a strong personal motivation for my work. The challenge, though, is that agile coaches are not well equipped or trained on how to have conversations relating to purpose or WILL.

Agile coaches sometimes need to work with their client's WILL or purpose as part of their role to enable the adoption of agile ways of working. When facing resistance to change, coaches should be able to move conversations down to level 4: open WILL. This is highly rewarding work and brings meaning to an agile coaching role. Plus, it serves the client. So how do coaches take the conversation down to this level? This answer is, very carefully, with absolute orientation to serve the client and by asking the right questions while holding the space.

It is here that agile coaching and professional coaching start to overlap; I'll show how they can be utilized in combination in chapter 12 where I compare agile and professional coaching, but for now I'd like to focus your attention on some simple, easy to ask, open WILL questions that you can practice.

Key question: "What do *you* have to let go of to make room for new ways to work?"

The above question is combined with the use of **silence.**

The coach in this situation is aiming to have the client realize that in order to move forward and Co-create the way of working with the coach, they have to let go of something. This something is usually an idea, belief, habit, or way they are used to doing something that no longer serves them.

During a level-4 conversation, the agile coach is seeking to evoke presence—an atmosphere where the client feels so safe that they can take a step into the unknown and let new ideas, ways of working, habits, or a new sense of self emerge from the conversation. It is a generative environment where collective creativity occurs; it is a place that has no judgement from the coach and can only be entered into if all of the previously mentioned "do not dos" are adhered to.

As the conversation slows down, silence is the secret ingredient that enables all of this to come together. Silence is used after the coach asks the right question. The timing on when to stop talking is something I cannot give you a formula for; you need to practice, experiment, try, and fail to learn when the time is right to ask one more question and when you just need to be quiet and let silence do the work for you.

Here are some other questions that help evoke presence and bring the client towards open WILL:

> "So, what has to change here?"
>
> "What's emerging here?"
>
> "What has this got to do with you and your role?"
>
> "What is missing here for you to move forward?"
>
> "What has to change for you?"
>
> "What's all this got to do with how you work?"
>
> "What do you need to let go of to make room for what is to come?"

When coaching teams, simply change the examples above to "we/us" questions.

Remember, it is important to pause, slow down the conversation's pace, and hold back your expert mindset from inserting ideas, opinion, thoughts, suggestions, judgements, or challenging "why" questions into the conversation.

In the silence, when the client is pondering the answer to a question, what does the agile coach do? Simple; Await. You sit there with an open MIND, open HEART, and open WILL in total service to the client, paying absolute attention to what they are about to say next, not with a view of analyzing it or judging it but ready to support the client to work their way forward towards to the next step in the Responsive Agile Coaching model: Co-create. It is here that you're gently moving the client forward into action. Small, achievable steps towards better ways of working.

Chapter Summary

- Open and Hold is by far the most difficult move in the Responsive Agile Coaching model; it is where the coach enables most of the deep change to occur.

- This move requires the coach to open their MIND, HEART, and WILL first; then the client will follow and be open to change. The coach leads the way for the client.

- The coach must have a genuine intent to serve during this move; otherwise, the client's intuition will sense that the conversation is inauthentic and psychologically unsafe.

- Holding the space is a critical capability the agile coach must develop to be able to execute the Open and Hold move.

- To hold the space an agile coach must keep all of their ideas, opinions, solutions, or judgments out of the conversation.

- Open WILL conversations are not always required, but agile coaches should be prepared to take the conversation down to this level if it serves the client.

CHAPTER 10.

MOVE 4: AWAIT THEN CO-CREATE (AND EMBED)

How to "Await"

To execute this step in the move, you must have patience. Awaiting as part of the Responsive Agile Coaching model is defined as: *"To have something in the future waiting for you."*

What's this "something" waiting in the future? The answer is a better way to work, a new sense of self, and/or a new sense of purpose (WILL). This step in the Await and Co-create move comes at what could be considered the "bottom" of the "down" pathway. Think back to Chapter 6, when I introduced you to what was called a level-4 conversation involving "collective creativity." Well, in the Await step you are in the "pause" before the Co-creation step, prior to the creative process starting.

This step is special in that it is more about what not to do. Rather than asking lots of questions like in previous moves, the coach uses silence, sharpens their awareness, and maintains a state of readiness, *awaiting* for emergence of the new ideas in the moment. Awaiting is not about having the perfect question to complete the move but staying alert and paying atten-

tion to the future that is emerging in the conversation.

If you have conducted the previous Open and Hold move well, then the client will feel safe to open up and explore new ways to work with you. When this is happening, the client will often have a moment where they start to imagine the way forward; often the first sign is that their tone of voice changes and you notice their willingness to explore what "could be." This indicates they have "let go" of old thoughts and ideas and are ready to "let come" new ways to work and be.

It is during this part of the conversation that the agile coach patiently awaits what is about to come. The risk for the coach is they shut down the conversation space by giving their opinion or suggestions too early; this is not how to Await.

The agile coach should encourage the client to keep *their* ideas flowing in this step. Questions that can be used as part of this step in the move include:

"And what else?"

"Interesting, tell me more"

"That's great. And what other options do we have?"

Once you start to see new ideas about ways of working start to form, it is your signal to move the conversation towards the Co-create step of the move.

Co-create Questions

This step in the Responsive Agile Coaching model is named co-creation because it is important that the coach creates a better agile way to work *with* the client. It is a collaborative effort. The coach works with the client, who now has an open mind and is in a safe space to try a new habit, behavior, or agile practice.

The Co-create step is an important meeting point where the client's previous resistance to change has been transformed into positive energy to collaborate with the coach. The result is a way to work that is not the coach's idea or opinion but a collectively created way of working that is accepted by the client because they helped design it.

The coach helps generate options and alternative ways to work but anchors their ideas on what came out of the conversation with the client, introducing their experience and ideas but always in alignment with the conversation that has preceded the co-creation step. But even though the agile coach can now contribute their ideas into the conversation, it does not mean they can simply adopt an expert mindset and provide the answer they had before the conversation started. The coach offers their ideas to the client in order to Co-create the way forward together. The best outcomes happen when the coach "lets go" of their opinion and solution and genuinely accepts the client's ideas into the way forward.

The most important coaching tip is to ensure everyone in the conversation focuses their attention on these two aspects:

1. Looking for indications of the emerging future; these start off as feelings or "off-the-cuff" comments about what the

way forward could look like. For example, "Maybe we could just..." or "What if we just..." can easily be ignored if the coach is not carefully listening.

2. Holding the space or atmosphere and ensuring it continues to be safe and non-judgmental. All of the guidelines I gave in the open Mind section still apply here to ensure the coach does not disrupt the flow of the creative conversation.

As the new way of working is forming up in the conversation and the coach and client are discussing what tangible steps will be taken, it is important to be iterative. Whatever is being proposed as the next change to behavior should be small, implemented quickly, tested, and then feedback should be sought. Then you iterate again, test and learn, and then repeat together.

Key question: "What's our way forward here?"

Or "What's the smallest best next step for us to move forward?"

After asking this question, let the client give their response, let them talk, and once you sense the timing is right, make a contribution. Done well, this is simply a continuation of the dialogue created previously; done poorly, it just starts a debate again and you're back to where you started the conversation. So, tread carefully with providing your contribution to the conversation as you Co-create the way forward with the client.

Additional questions to help Co-create could be:

"What is the best first step forward?"

"What experiment could we run to test our thinking here?"

"What's a safe first step that feels right?"

"What do we want to try?"

Here are a few suggested ways to contribute to the conversation as the agile coach:

"What's coming up for me as we talk is…"

"What do you think of…"

"Can I offer something for us to consider?"

"I've noticed this seems to be a common theme in our conversation…"

In this step of the conversation, ideas are flowing, and actions are being planned but with a common sense of purpose and consensus. Usually, in this step of the coaching conversation, things are flowing quickly, and it seems like this almost takes care of itself. Be careful not to get complacent. A good agile coach will ensure that, after the breakthrough moment and once co-creation is in motion, an agreed way forward is documented in some way. Often in the excitement, things can get lost and in the subsequent days forgotten or misrepresented.

As you practice working across the four levels of conversation, you'll notice how they are not linear. Sometimes you circle between levels as the conversation flows, and that's expected, so just go with it. But remember to always keep track of where you are and attempt to enable the client to move forward; that's coaching. Staying in long, deep conversations without moving forward is wasteful and is not coaching.

Embed Questions

As the conversation moves into the end point in the model, the agile coach is aiming to turn a small change in the way of working into an ongoing behavior. Often these questions are in subsequent conversations, but, regardless, an attempt to embed a behavior should be made by the coach where possible. This is about making the new behavior stick.

Key question: "What did you learn from the change?"

Or some additional suggestions include:

"I observed this last sprint; what did you see as a team that is different?"

"How do you think we're progressing with our move to agile?"

"I'd like to point out <<*insert improvement here*>>; this is a great result!"

Adoption of agile is all about learning loops—feedback loops from trying something new and then doing a retrospective assessment of the results. Questions from the coach should follow this model and ask the client what they are learning from the changes they are experimenting with. As the coach and client co-create new agile ways to work, they should be asking each other what they learned periodically. If no one is asking this question, then it is the coach's job to ask it and encourage others to ask the same question of themselves and to their teams.

A sure sign that embedding has occurred is what happens when no one is looking (i.e., the coach is not there). Periodic "coaching back" is recommended; check in and see if the way of working is still maturing or is stagnating for past clients.

One way I accelerate embedding is by pointing out (to the team) the difference in where the team is now compared to where they used to be, usually at retrospectives. As I point out the team's improvements, I always include data from any observations, assessments, surveys, polls, or similar tools I utilize as a coach to monitor team performance/culture. I use a combination of quantitative assessments combined with qualitative surveys to do this. I don't use this data outside of the team; if you do this, it becomes a management tool and will almost certainly lead to your data collection being gamified by the team.

To achieve an embedding outcome with individuals, I use real-time feedback; acknowledging a team member's extra effort to collaborate, for example. This public praise when combined with private coaching is a powerful embedding tool that, when done consistently, can turn small gains into larger changes across a team.

One important point is to be careful to not claim you have embedded too early. I think the real test of embedding is when people come under pressure to deliver; does the way of working "hold" or does it buckle under the strain of expectation? I recently had an example of this. A team of agile coaches had just finished a 16-week engagement for a product team; they delivered their coaching service summary report containing evidence of all the practices that had been adopted by the teams. The problems started as the product launch date approached. The coaches had all moved on, but when the product launch window approached, the teams reverted back to chaos. I spoke to a scrum master, who told me everyone panicked and stopped writing user stories; no one attended any ceremonies to help plan or collaborate on the work. This was a great reminder of testing that the Embed step is complete prior to concluding a coaching engagement.

Chapter Summary

* In the Await step, the agile coach needs to look for what is emerging during the conversation; these might be "weak signals" but should be followed if it feels right. Silence is the key here; do not provide your ideas as you Await.

* The co-creation element of the "Await then Co-create" move is a joint, collaborative activity between the coach and the client; the coach must refrain from falling into becoming the expert and telling the client.

* An iterative approach is best when co-creating; small, safe steps are best to experiment the way forward to better ways of working.

* Embedding aims to make sure the way of working has "stuck"; a good test is to see what happens when the coach is not there. Positive feedback helps accelerate embedding. Coaching back is a good way to check in on previous clients to ensure the way of working is continuing to improve in the coach's absence or when the pressure to deliver is on.

CHAPTER 11.

RESPONSIVE AGILE COACHING – ONE-ON-ONE

After taking you through all the steps and moves in the model, I'd like to now demonstrate how a typical responsive agile coaching conversation could flow when coaching a single person. My aim in doing this is to make it real and show how the sum of all the parts can come together into a coherent flow between coach and client.

The scenario I'll use is constructed from a real conversation I had with a client. In this example the senior coach here is Sarah, the junior agile coach is Ross, and the client is a product owner called Nigel. The scene is the launch of a large agile program; all the teams have come together for the first time, and Nigel is with his team to create a team charter.

Sense and Respond

Ross was new to agile coaching and was keen to make an impression at the launch event; he wanted to have his team see him as a person who can help and solve problems. Unfortunately, things had not gotten off to a great start.

"Geez, Nigel is so commanding and controlling; he's basically standing in the middle of his team, telling everyone what the team charter is going to have in it," Ross said to one of his fellow coaches, Nicki.

"Yes, he is not letting anyone else use the whiteboard marker and is controlling the conversation; you can tell, as three of his team have disengaged and are talking in a huddle to the side," Nicki responded as a they watched Nigel frantically attempting to get input for the charter from his somewhat reluctant team.

"I'm going to say something; he needs to be more collaborative," Ross said, seeing an opportunity to coach.

"Sure, go ahead, but he looks a bit stressed out," Nicki observed.

Across Pathway – an Attempt to Tell or Show

Ross walked over and into the middle of the team and said, "Hi, everyone. I'm Ross, your agile coach. Is everyone here contributing? Do you need me to help facilitate?"

Nicki, watching on, noticed Nigel's facial expression; it seemed to be a mix of resentment and disappointment.

"Ross, we're OK. Just give us some space to figure this out please," Nigel said.

Ross walked away, feeling a little rejected and somewhat shamed in front of his peer, Nicki. "Well, that went well!" Ross said as he let out a deep breath.

Just then, the senior agile coach, Sarah, came over to check in on Ross. "Hi, Ross; interesting dynamic I notice in your team. Have you heard of the saying 'he who holds the pen has the power'?"

Ross replied, "Oh, yes, Nigel is holding the pen (whiteboard marker) and the power, controlling the creation of the team charter; hence, there's low collaboration."

"Exactly!" Sarah replied. Before she could continue, Ross somewhat defensively said, "Well, we've tried to get Nigel to listen, but he essentially told us to go away."

Sarah sensed Ross' frustration and decided to try an experiment to help Ross and Nicki learn through observation.

Down Pathway – Open and Hold

Sarah walked over to Nigel and his team. She stepped next to Nigel and quietly and privately spoke to him: "Hi, Nigel. I'm Sarah; I work as one of the senior agile coaches supporting Ross; have you got a couple of minutes to talk?"

Nigel looked apprehensive; the voice in his head started talking to him at a hundred miles an hour. *Am I doing something wrong? I'm so nervous about messing this up on this first day with the team. I hope this coach is not going to make me look incompetent!*

Nigel looked a little bit like a deer in the headlights; he was frozen on the spot with a panicked look on his face. Sarah indicated for him to come away from the team for a moment as they continued the conversation.

Sarah noticed Nigel was not comfortable as they moved away from the team; she leaned in and spoke so no one else could hear: "Are you OK, Nigel? I just want to check in on you."

Nigel was silent and didn't respond, but he let out a sigh and his shoulders dropped a few inches.

As Sarah and Nigel rejoined Nicki and Ross, Sarah said, "Thanks for taking a moment, Nigel; all I wanted to do was say that we are all here to make you and your team successful; that's it. That is our only job today. We're here to serve you as you learn about all of this agile stuff." Sarah then continued, "And, Nigel, it is really important for you to understand that you are not expected to know everything or get it 'right'; it is OK for us all to do this together."

Sarah paused briefly to let what she'd said register with Nigel. He seemed to be considering what to say but was struggling to talk.

Sarah orientated herself; she sensed Nigel was at his limit emotionally, so she decided to ask about his role. "So how is it going for you in your new role, Nigel?"

Awaiting

After asking this question, Sarah was then quiet and made eye contact with Ross and Nicki, indicating they should be quiet and wait for Nigel's response.

Nigel replied, "Well, we are getting organized and should get the charter done in time—"

Sarah politely interrupted: "Sorry, Nigel, I really just want to know how *you* are doing. Right now I'm not concerned about the charter or your team; for the moment, it's you I want to support."

There was a noticeable silence, a pause as Nigel took in what Sarah had just said; it seemed to have deeply affected him.

Upon hearing this, Nigel became visibly emotional. He didn't respond immediately. *No one has ever asked me how I'm doing and really cared about the answer.* He considered how to reply to Sarah.

"Well, there's a lot to learn, and to be honest, I'm a bit overwhelmed with all the new agile language, processes, etc.," Nigel shared, his voice quivering with emotion.

Sarah considered what to do next in the coaching conversation. Nigel was obviously overwhelmed and struggling. She decided to acknowledge Nigel's openness and conclude the conversation for now.

"Nigel, it is great you were so open with us. We're a team here. Ross, specifically, is here all day, so reach out as you need to."

Co-create

Nigel thanked Sarah and returned to his team. Nicki, Ross, and Sarah had a quick debrief huddle.

"Ross, I'm hoping you noticed the moves I made in that coaching conversation."

"You sought permission to coach, your orientation to serve was made explicit, you then opened the space and held it for the emotion that Nigel was showing."

"Yes; spot on, Ross. What I suggest you do is reconnect with Nigel privately when the timing is right and continue the conversation to help co-create the way of working with him and his team."

Embed

Later in the day, Sarah checked back in with Ross. "Hi, Ross. How did things go with Nigel?"

"Well, after your 'intervention,' he seemed to be much less defensive and open to working with me. We actually did the backlog creation together with the team and have estimated the first sprint for next week. It's like what you did built his trust from zero to a lot in five minutes," Ross said admiringly.

"Well, when people are not used to genuine authentic conversations, it can take them by surprise and have a big effect on them," Sarah responded.

Epilogue to this story: This is a real example, and just before we finalized this chapter for the book editors, I was told by one of the agile coaches that Nigel has received a recognition award from the scrum master community for his openness to learning and willingness to embrace new ways of working.

Chapter Summary

+ Agile coaching conversations are dynamic; through the different moves, the parts of the Responsive Agile Coaching model connect together into a coherent, flowing conversation.

CHAPTER 12.

RESPONSIVE VERSUS PROFESSIONAL COACHING

Overview of the GROW model

Before I move on and take you through how the Responsive Agile Coaching model can be applied to a team, I'd like to dedicate a chapter for a discussion on how professional coaching (as previously defined in Chapter 3) aligns with the Responsive Agile Coaching model. This is important because the two are not mutually exclusive and are, in fact, complimentary. It is not within the scope of this book for me to go into great detail on professional coaching, but I do want to show you how agile and professional coaching fit together within Responsive Agile Coaching.

The most popular model in professional coaching is the GROW model.[4] GROW stands for:

- **Goal:** What is the goal for the coaching session?

- **Reality:** Helping the client re-see their situation and separate opinion from fact.

- **Options:** Generate multiple ideas through co-creative conversation.

- **Way forward:** Agree on what the client is going to do after leaving the conversation.

The GROW model maps neatly onto the downward pathway of the Responsive Agile Coaching model as shown in the diagram on the next page. Let me take you through how the two models can work together.

Using GROW with Responsive Agile Coaching

I've considered how the GROW model can be utilized by agile coaches; it is not as simple as learning how to have a professional coaching GROW conversation and "bolting" it onto your agile coaching practice. There's a better way to implement GROW as an agile coach. Let me explain with a quick review of what an agile coach actually does when they are at the Responsive Moment. They're making a choice to follow the down pathway with an Open and Hold move or go across with the Tell or Show move. The GROW model supports the Open and Hold move of the downward pathway. Below I'll explain each stage of the GROW model and provide additional ideas for how you can utilize it in combination with the Responsive Agile Coaching model.

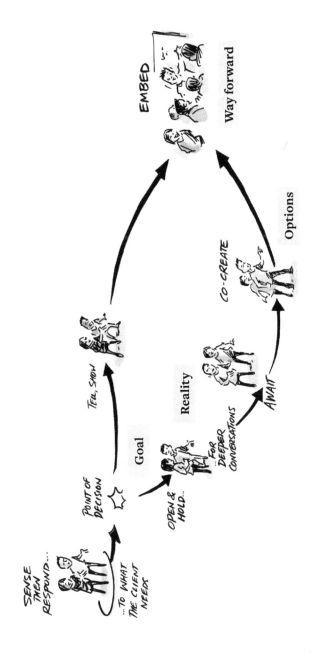

SENSE THEN RESPOND...

...TO WHAT THE CLIENT NEEDS

POINT OF DECISION

Goal

TELL, SHOW

OPEN & HOLD...

...FOR DEEPER CONVERSATIONS

Reality

AWAIT

CO-CREATE

Options

EMBED

Way forward

Goal

Both models will have a point where a "goal" for the coaching conversation needs to be ascertained. In using the GROW model, this is a formal, structured, and exploratory dialogue between the coach and client. In responsive agile coaching, a goal is important but may not always be discussed openly between coach/client; it may not be an explicit point of conversation. Nonetheless, the agile coach will have a goal in mind as they proceed to start a conversation with a client. Agile coaching has an overarching goal to implement agile as a way to work whereas professional coaching has goals that are more driven by the client's individual personal issues.

Reality

In a GROW-model conversation, the exploration of "reality" is structured and in the form of an open dialogue between coach/client; this is quite similar to Open and Hold move, where the agile coach supports the client to "re-see" the facts and identify emotions that are at play. Both models support a shared understanding of what is real for the client in terms of emotions and facts relating to a situation.

Options

Exploring "options" before choosing a way forward is a key aspect of the GROW model. This maps neatly into the Await and Co-create steps of the Responsive Agile Coaching model. Generating options is less prevalent in the Tell or Show move of the across pathway, where the agile coach provides answers instead of generating options.

Way Forward

The "way forward" in GROW is closely aligned with the Co-create and Embed steps of the Responsive Agile Coaching model. Often a professional coach will explicitly ask for and obtain a commitment from a client to trying a new behavior or doing some "homework" as part of finalizing the "way forward" at the conclusion of a GROW coaching session. In agile coaching, the commitments made by clients usually do not have as much weight or level of personal accountability to the agile coach from the client. Often an agile coach is recommending or advising and may not seek a commitment from the client.

Responsive versus Professional Coaching – Key Differences

Although there are many similarities between the GROW and Responsive Agile coaching models, there are also some key differences, namely:

1. GROW conversations are structured, formal, and private/confidential. Agile coaching is often more informal, less structured, and "in the moment" and may not always be confidential.

2. The Tell or Show move in the Responsive Agile Coaching model has less consideration for exploring deep dialogue and is more transactional between the coach and client.

Tell or Show is more like instruction and training than coaching, even if it is part of an overall Responsive Agile Coaching model.

3. The goals of GROW coaching conversations are almost exclusively client-centric; whereas in Responsive Agile Coaching, goals are more skewed towards achievement of organizational change outcomes related to adoption of ways of working.

4. The Responsive Agile Coaching model is based on Theory U and the work from The Presencing Institute; it is designed to enable dialogue between people, including deep, empathetic listening and sensing for personal and collective purposes. The GROW model, on the other hand, is a generic conversation guide that helps coaches set goals with clients; it does not specifically advise on how to conduct transformative conversations with clients.

Chapter Summary

+ The down pathway of the Responsive Agile Coaching model closely aligns with the professional coaching GROW model.

+ Key differences between GROW and Responsive Agile Coaching include GROW focusing almost exclusively on the client's goal and GROW coaching being more structured, confidential, and formal in nature.

CHAPTER 13.

RESPONSIVE AGILE COACHING WITH A TEAM

Accelerating Coaching Outcomes

Most agile coaching is done at the team level; probably 80 percent. But how do we actually coach a team to adopt agile and achieve high levels of performance using the Responsive Agile Coaching model?

As agile coaches we have the job of enabling teams to implement better ways of working, but we have limited time to get this done. In fact, from my experience, the best coaches get this done faster than average coaches. In order to coach an agile team to high performance in the shortest possible time, the agile coach should have a strategy or approach. Randomly throwing ideas or moves at a team won't work; in fact, it could make their performance deteriorate. In Chapter 5, I outlined three elements required for change to stick:

1. Individual psychological: *helping individuals change their behaviors and mindsets.*

2. Social: *holding teams accountable to agreed norms/behaviors.*

3. Structural processes: *implementing an agile framework and associated processes.*

I'd like to address these three points as they relate to change management of agile into a team's way of working. The two tools from the agile coach's bag that help form the strategy I'm about to show you, are the use of a social contract (point 2) and your agreed agile framework (point 3). These are combined with individual coaching for team members (point 1) to provide us with an overall change management strategy.

My experience in consulting has taught me that you need to be able to apply a strategy together with a coaching model to quickly deliver change into a team. Below is my strategy that combines change management and agile frameworks with the Responsive Agile Coaching model to accelerate your ability to achieve coaching outcomes.

Coaching a Team from Forming to Performing

Usually the first retrospective with a newly formed team is a polite but somewhat awkward affair. If you have ever facilitated a retrospective with a new team and attempted to have an open and deep conversation with them, you are usually met with silence. Additionally, if the team is offshore or you are facilitating remotely, then it is even harder to have open conversations and discuss any pain points or dysfunctions the team may have. This is normal and is part of the "forming" stage in Tuckman's original four stages of group development (1. Forming; 2. Storming; 3. Norming; 4. Performing).[5] Here is a summary if you're unfamiliar with this model.

Tuckman Stage explanation

FORMING

Team is newly formed, getting to know each other. Often during this stage team members are polite and do not challenge each other.

STORMING

Disagreement and conflict happen as the team stop being polite and openly discuss how to work with each other. This stage may have inter-personal conflict as the team members argue their differences of opinion.

NORMING

The team starts to settle on what it is that they collectively agree are their shared norms, values and behaviors. Team members hold each other to account for following the agreed way to behave.

PERFORMING

Team gets on with the work; outcomes/outputs flow, conflict is reduced and constructive dialogue starts. The team resolve issues quickly and collectively.

Before I share my ideas on how you can help agile teams to accelerate to the "perform" stage, I need to update you with some recent research on how Tuckman's stages have actually been found to apply in real-life settings. In short, most teams are always storming to some degree; it is not really a stage and can be continuous. This means you will need a coaching approach to help deal with the energy associated with team storming. It is important to be able to deal with this storming energy while also helping the team form, norm, and perform. Let me show you how to do this.

Tuckman's Stages (Modified) for Agile Team Coaching

I want to use a modified version of Tuckman's stages to show you how I coach agile teams using the moves in the Responsive Agile Coaching model. Why modified? Let me explain. An extensive literature review of Tuckman's model was undertaken by researcher Denise Bonebright, where she concluded that Tuckman's model still (after 40 years of use) has the most utility at "providing a simple, accessible starting point for conversations about key issues of group dynamics."[6]

In summary, Bonebright confirms that Tuckman's model is great at helping us have a common language on how teams behave. But other research points to some modifications that better explain what happens in reality. I would like to focus on a couple of papers. Firstly, I want to point out a very thorough piece of research by Pamela Knight titled "Acquisition Community Team Dynamics: The Tuckman Model vs. the DAU Model." The key findings in this paper were:

- Teams continually storm (it is not a stage).
- Forming is a distinctive phase at the start.
- After forming, teams move into a mix of norming and performing stages.[7]

If we were to graphically represent these findings, they would look something like this:

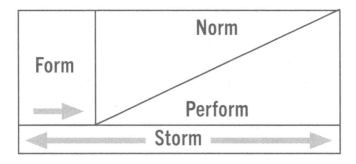

Other research by Kate Cassidy supports the above illustration, with findings that indicate "variation in the location and definition of the conflict stage." [8]

The reason I am making so big a point about conflict and the storming stage in (agile) team development is because as coaches our job is to manage, deal with, and utilize the energy associated with storming and channel it into positive change to improve team performance. So how do agile coaches channel this energy from storming? Simple; use a container.

Why "Containers" Are Critical to Coaching Agile Teams

"What is able to come 'through' a group of people depends directly on the strength of their container."

—Kelvy Bird, Presencing Institute

The concept of a container for agile coaching is a useful metaphor to illustrate how we hold the space for an agile team as they storm, norm, and perform. Think of the container keeping the energy that is generated from storming from spilling out and becoming overly disruptive to the team as they attempt to form and norm. It is our job to enable the creation of this container. "How?" you ask. I see two parts to the agile coaching team container:

1. **The agile framework**: scrum, Kanban, and other associated agile practices.

2. **Team psychological safety**: defined as being able to show and employ one's self without fear of negative consequences of self-image, status, or career.[7]

An agile framework is used to coach "against" and hold the team to an agreed (initial) way to do work together. Essentially, it is these frameworks that bring order and prevent the team from falling into chaos (maybe a bit dramatic, but you get the idea). One way to think of this is that the framework does the coaching for you. Instead of having 10 conversations with each individual team member, the agreed framework allows you to Tell or Show the whole team at the same time and have a common starting point for your agile coaching work. This is often what training or lunchtime learning sessions allow an agile coach to do: create the framework part of the container with all team members at the same time.

When we are coaching larger systems of work (trains, tribes, or teams of agile teams up to 200 people), there are scaling frameworks that provide us with a container. Some of my more challenging coaching engagements have happended where I've been working at scale, but the "container" framework had not been agreed. What resulted were endless arguments on such things as what to call the different sized product backlog items (epic versus feature naming conventions, for example). Additionally, roles and responsibilities need to be defined for scaled delivery; this is a non-trivial undertaking, and if you start coaching without these having been agreed, your job is significantly more challenging as excessive conflict (storming) distracts everyone from getting on with delivering value.

So, my advice is be clear—really clear—on your framework and agreed (initial) starting point for the way of working. If you don't have this agreed, you risk the levels of storming becoming excessive and lasting indefinitely; you may never get to norming or performing. Don't laugh; I've seen this (more than once).

Finally, I must reinforce the criticality of creating and maintaining psychological safety in the team. This part of the container is equally as important as your framework. This starts with the creation of a social contract/team charter during the forming stage and then subsequent coaching to ensure team members adhere to the agreed behavioral norms (even as they storm). Creating, keeping, and reinforcing this safety is the coach's job. You will work with the whole team, small groups, and individuals to hold everyone accountable for their behavior. This creates the safety; but remember, safety can be undone very quickly, so you need to be vigilant as the team forms.

Together these two elements will provide you with the ability to contain the energy of the team as they progress and mature. Let's now consider what this progress looks like using a modified version of Tuckman's development model.

An Agile Team Change Management Approach

Below is a summary of each Tuckman stage together with a three-phase approach I use when coaching agile teams; it also shows you how the different moves of the Responsive Agile Coaching model could be utilized.

The aim of the above table is to provide you with ideas and suggestions; it is not a prescriptive method, just a guide. Below I've provided some more details on each phase to help you consider how you might implement some of these ideas into your responsive agile coaching practice.

Phase	Tuckman Stage	How to utilize Moves
1. Create the container The coach uses an agile framework to put boundaries around team behavior and bring order through shared understanding.	**FORMING** (Team is newly formed, getting to know each other)	Elements of Responsive Agile Coaching model: **Sense then Respond, Tell or Show** After a period of sensing to understand the situation, the agile coach usually Tells or Shows the team an agile framework. This provides a container to support the team as they form. This could be scrum and/or other agile frameworks and associated practices. Be clear about the agreed first iteration of the way of working, document it and ensure everyone is on the same page. During the phase the coach should facilitate the creation of a social contract and/or team charter to enable the team to agree on a shared set of norms; this starts to create psychological safety.
2. Resolve resistance Within the container provided by the agile framework, the coach deals with resistance.	**NORMING** (Team start to settle on what it is that they collectively agree are their shared norms, values and behaviors)	Elements of Responsive Agile Coaching model: **Sense then Respond, Open and Hold** As the team "bounces against the container" there will be conflict and resistance; this is expected and part of norming. During this stage the coach keeps reminding the team of the social contract and supports open team conversations through holding the space (mantaining safety). Await and Co-create steps will come into play here as the coach deals with resistance from some strong personalities within the team.
3. Embed/ re-provoke The coach works to establish norms of behavior through dialogue, co-creation and embedding.		Elements of Responsive Agile Coaching model: **Await and Co-create** The team starts to get used to having open conversations; the more they have them, the faster they get to the norm stage. Teams may get stuck in excessive storming if the coach does not support the team to have Open and Hold conversations together. Retrospectives and other ad-hoc coaching activity are the best way to do this. Positive reinforcement is given for behavior that is in line with the social contract.
	PERFORMING (Team gets on with the work; outcomes/ output flow as conflict is replaced with constructive dialogue)	Elements of Responsive Agile Coaching model: **Embed** The change implemented through the previous stages should now be embedded. Embedding continues in this phase as the coach starts to step back from the team and let them be, only coaching back occasionally. Because agile adoption is never "done" the coach is continuously provoking the team to improve. This is usually achieved by being direct; using Tell or Show.

Second column spanning label: CONTINUOUS STORMING — Coach needs create and maintain the container for the team whilst it forms/norms (Levels of team conflict vary across all stages. Coach needs create and maintain the container for the team whilst it forms/norms)

Phase One – Create the Container

In this 4- to 6-week phase, the coach spends a lot of their time establishing the agreed/chosen framework or elements/ patterns of an agile framework. As an agile coach commences an engagement, there is usually an expectation that they will Tell or Show the team what they should be doing. A coach's first move is usually Tell or Show, and this is OK. By showing the team what to do, it brings some order from chaos, especially if agile is new for the team. This helps everyone be less panicked and feel some safety in knowing there is a process. I call this "creating the container" for the system of work. The container will involve one of the many agile frameworks; scrum, Kanban, for example. This phase utilizes the "agile" part of agile coaching, where your expertise/knowledge of agile is the main contribution to helping the team.

As I explained in the sunny-day scenario, as long the pre-requisites are in place and you are well sponsored, you should start telling the team what and how to do agile (and thus create your container). Your job in this phase is to ensure that the framework is adhered to so that people start to understand that these guardrails are not (at least to start with) up for discussion. This allows you to start to observe where any particular individuals in the team may be resisting the adoption of agile practices. When you encounter resistance, this is where the Open and Hold move comes into play. During phase one, you will usually facilitate Open and Hold conversations with the entire team during the creation of the social contract or team charter document as well as during the retrospectives as they occur periodically. This will ensure you're building psychological safety as you implement the framework.

It is not uncommon, especially for new teams, that the initial Open and Hold conversations are awkward and difficult; the team does not know each other yet and they are uncertain whether the environment is psychologically safe for them to be vulnerable. A team member is not going to share what is on their mind or how they feel or why they come to work with people they don't know; it takes two or three sprints for the team to form and get to this point. And it is the agile coach's job to hold the space for the team and build safety.

Phase Two – Resolve Resistance

During this second 4- to 6-week phase, you start to have coaching sessions with small subgroups of the team, usually by role, as well as one-on-one conversations.

When working in these smaller groups and because you are discussing the way of working with people doing the same role, it makes it easier to facilitate deeper and more open conversations about the issues they're facing. During these conversations, you will be holding the space for the team members to share what is on their minds and how they feel while assessing their level of motivation and purpose. This is also the time to ensure everyone is following the agreed norms in the social contract; if they are not, then Open and Hold the space for a deeper conversation and Co-create a way forward.

You should be using insights from these small group conversations as well as individual one-on-one conversations to start to prepare a coaching backlog to address the themes/pain points in the team and enable them to progress toward the norming stage.

It is important to only commence the Open and Hold move after the container is in place. Why? Well, the container does most of the work for the coach. By telling the team how and what to do, the coach does not have to convince (individually coach) every person, one at a time. If, to start with, the team rejects what you tell them is the best framework to start with, you may not be sponsored strongly enough, you could be struggling with establishing credibility, or you're implementing too many changes too quickly. If this happens, take a step back and reassess your approach and pace.

Phase Three - Embed and Re-provoke

During phase 3, the coach will be embedding the work done in the previous two phases. There will be lots of positive reinforcement; even small gains should be openly and publicly celebrated as the team starts to embed change. This phase is ongoing until the coaching engagement ends. The work done utilizing the Tell or Show moves in phase one together with the co-created outcomes from the Open and Hold conversations in phase two both contribute to improvements that now have to be embedded into the team's way of working.

I think if an agile coach can reach phase three in 12 weeks, then they've done a good job. The best agile coaches know how to accelerate the team to the "performing" stage quickly. It is my opinion that the ability to achieve accelerated outcomes is due to a coach's ability to be responsive; take the downward pathway as required with the team, subgroups, and individuals.

Novice agile coaches are often over reliant on Telling or Showing, and results tend to be superficial because too much unresolved conflict remains. Without being able to have the deeper conversations required for dealing with resistance within the team, the novice coach finds they are still attempting to resolve team dysfunctions many weeks after starting an engagement. One mitigation for this is ensuring you always have a mentor to observe you work and act as a sounding board.

Finally, it is in this phase that the agile coach will re-provoke the team to ensure they don't settle too much. Continuously striving for higher levels of performance should be the goal here; you're never "done" with improving your agile way of working.

Chapter Summary

- A three-phase change management approach is provided to help agile coaches move their teams towards high-performance; 1. Create the Container, 2. Resolve Resistance and 3. Embed/Re-provoke.

- The moves in the Responsive Agile Coaching model can be combined with the three-phase change approach to accelerate teams through a modified version of Tuckman's four stages of group development.

- Twelve weeks is a reasonable amount of time for an agile coach to take a team through to the Perform stage. To achieve this, the prerequisites for an agile coaching engagement need to be in place, especially strong sponsorship.

CHAPTER 14.

COMBINATIONS AND EXPERIMENTATION

N ow that I've taken you through how to conduct respon- sive agile coaching conversations, I want to outline my thinking on how the moves and steps can be combined together. There is value in practicing the model as I've outlined it, but I wanted you to understand that it should be applied with an experimental test and learn mindset—not dogmatically adhered to.

Provocation in Your First Encounter

Provocation is something I've been told (through lots of "feedback") that I'm highly capable at executing. Provocation is defined in a somewhat negative light by the dictionary as "stimulate or give rise to a reaction or emotion, (typically a strong or unwelcome one) in someone".

The balance between provoking your client and just plain annoying them is a fine line but one that I think needs to be walked during an agile coaching engagement.

As you progress through the three phases I outlined in the previous chapter, you are also attempting to evoke a reaction or response from the client/s so you can learn what to do next (choose your pathway, make a move, or take a step). The data you get when you provoke a client is critical in determining your next move, so it is important to turn up your sensing capability after a provocation.

The takeaway message here is don't be afraid to cause a little disruption and perturb your clients, especially if they're holding on too tightly to the status quo. This becomes important once you've established your container (basic agile framework and a level of safety).

Cycling Between Tell and Open

Responsiveness in your agile coaching means you have developed the ability to switch or cycle between different moves; from Telling (giving clients safety in knowing) to a provocation followed by an Open move (to see what comes or emerges in the silence). Brad Bennet, Founder of EPiC Agile, an Australian agile transformation coaching company and one of the contributors to this book, calls this "leaning in and leaning out." Brad would even go as far as asking his clients how they were experiencing his work and if he was leaning in too much—like a temperature check to see if he was over-provoking. Try it as an experiment and as a means to moderate the amount of change you attempt to introduce to a team at any one time.

Other Moves and Combinations to Experiment With

The Responsive Agile Coaching model seems to flow along pathways and is neatly arranged, but this does not mean you rigidly apply it. Similar to the GROW (goal-reality-options-way forward) model of professional coaching, the responsive model is used by coaches to help navigate client conversations by enabling the coach to know where they are at any point in time. If you know where you are, you will be able to navigate the conversation forward towards an outcome. The real benefit of using coaching models is not to dogmatically adhere to the steps, moves, or pathways but to utilize them as a map to help you navigate (keep you from getting lost) during a coaching conversation.

Once you have become skilled in the basics of conversation, try some of the following move combinations:

Move combinations:

- Rapid cycles of Tell then Open. This alternates between provoking the client into thinking differently, then Opening the space for co-creation.

- Try an Open move, wait in silence for an uncomfortable amount of time, then, even if the client says nothing, attempt to start Co-creating by seeding an idea.

- After embedding, quickly provoke the client with a more advanced practice by assertively telling (just when they think it is safe to stop learning new/better ways to work).

- If you've been waiting in awkward silence for a while, offer to Show them (without telling).

- Show and never Tell is good for clients who learn by doing and don't respond as well to words.

- At the responsive moment, you can try any move or step to quickly test and learn; offer an idea to see if the client will take it, then switch to demonstrating something or use an open question about what they think is the answer. It is all about you (the coach) learning through the data you're collecting as you talk with clients.

- When sensing, check to see if the environment is right for you to make a subsequent move; often your timing may be wrong, meaning you should probably save your ideas for another time. As you practice your sensing, your timing will get more accurate, leading to faster results.

Practice the Basics, Experiment, Then Master

I remember when I first started to learn how to coach. I wanted so badly to be good at it that I attempted to take the coaching models I had been taught and immediately improve them (because I knew better). But I remember what my instructor and mentor at the time said to me, and it has stuck with me to this day:

> *"Master the basics or plain version of the model first, then once you have a good level of proficiency, you then start to add your 'flavorings' to the vanilla recipe."*

Putting your herbs and spices into a meal before you know how to cook it is not a good idea; you are changing too many variables at the same time. So, my advice is to become comfortable with the basic elements of the Responsive Agile Coaching model and learn to know where you are in a conversation at any point in time.

Once you've developed these skills, you can think about advanced moves and variations that you may think are a good idea. It is very important to make this model your own version—you need to coach with authenticity—but master the basics first. I suggest coaching "friendlies," who will give you feedback, first. This is a safe way for you to learn and improve rapidly.

Chapter Summary

- Variations should only be tried once you are proficient at utilizing the basics of the Responsive Agile Coaching model.

- Combinations of the different steps and moves provide agile coaches the opportunity to "mix and match" the different aspects of the Responsive Agile Coaching model to continuously challenge themselves and improve their coaching outcomes.

References and Further Reading

1. S.J. Segalowitz, "Knowing before we know: Conscious versus preconscious top–down processing and a neuroscience of intuition," *Brain and Cognition*, 65, no. 2 (November 2007): 143-144.

2. David Rock, Strategy+Business, organizations & people, Autumn 2009 / Issue 56.

3. Mary C. Lamia, "Like It or Not, Emotions Will Drive the Decisions You Make Today," *Psychology Today*, December 31, 2010, www.psychologytoday.com.

4. RUOK.org.au is the Australian charity that aims to reduce suicide rates through their initiatives.

5. Tuckman, Bruce W, "Developmental sequence in small groups". *Psychological Bulletin*. 1965, 63 (6): 384–399.

6. Kahn, William A, "Psychological Conditions of Personal Engagement and Disengagement at Work". *Academy of Management Journal.* 1990, 33 (4): 692–724.

7. Denise A. Bonebright, "40 years of storming: a historical review of Tuckman's model of small group development," *Human Resource Development International*, Vol. 13, No. 1, February 2010, 111–120.

8. Pamela Knight, "Acquisition Community Team Dynamics: The Tuckman Model vs. the DAU Model," *4th Annual Acquisition Research Symposium of the Naval Postgraduate School*, April 2007.

9. Cassidy, K. 2007. "Tuckman revisited: Proposing a new model of group development for practitioners." *Journal of Experiential Education* 29, no. 3: 413–7

10. Go to www.responsiveagile.coach to learn with others who have read or are reading this book; you can also visit www.responsiveagilecoaching.com for up-to-date content, downloads, and templates.

PART IV
RESPONSIVE AGILE COACHING PRACTICES

Introduction

Agile can be quite theoretical and abstract. Discussions on agile values, principles, and philosophies are prolific on the internet, with many heated arguments about who is right and who is wrong on some aspect of agile. Lately, I spend less time arguing about theory and more time working in the field with coaches on their practices. So, what is a practice? Here's a simple definition:

> *"The actual application or use of an idea, belief, or method, as opposed to theories relating to it."*

I wrote this book to provide you with a guiding script and associated set of practices on how agile coaching works. It is not prescriptive but is a guide to get you going and help you learn the pathways of agile coaching conversations. Beginners need some guidelines on how to do (practice) agile when they're starting, and the same applies for agile coaching. New coaches need to have a set of practices that apply coaching in the real world; the same as a tennis player needs to stop talking about hitting a ball and practice on the court.

Using questions is a practice; for agile coaches it is so important I focused an entire part of the book on how to ask the right question at the right time. What I'm going to take you through now are some other core practices that support great agile coaching conversations; let's start with listening.

CHAPTER 15.

KEY PRACTICE – LISTENING

If questions are the means to open up a coaching conversation, then it is listening that generates the content for the conversation. By listening, the agile coach is utilizing silence as a means to "hold the space" while the client considers and introspects. Listening also ensures the coach picks up on the right signs and signals during the conversation. If a coach cannot be silent and deeply listen, I would argue they're not a coach. Listening and silence are that important to agile coaching. There are different types/levels/depths of listening, and there are many models out there that define these, but my reference point comes from the Presencing Institute and their four-levels model.[1]

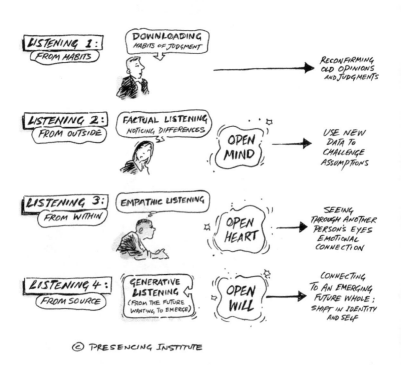

© PRESENCING INSTITUTE

Level 1 – When You Have the Right Answer

Level 1 – Downloading: This listening happens when a coach is downloading their expertise to the client. The coach is reconfirming *their* opinion by applying previously used solutions to a situation. Level-1 listening does not generate ideas with the client or leave room for the opinion of others.

Level 1 listening is quite superficial and is sometimes called "predatory" listening because the listener is really just waiting for a small gap in the conversation to jump in, pounce, and give their opinion; they're not really appreciating what the other person is saying.

Staying at this level is not recommended; agile coaches should seek to always move to level-2 listening, as it is where the coaching part of agile coaching starts to come into a conversation.

Level 2 – When Facts and Opinions Need to Be Heard

Level 2 – Factual: This listening should be the level that the agile coach keeps returning to; their home base. From here the conversation can proceed along any pathway; down or across. At level 2, the coach is starting to see and listen to the facts. The coach starts to see with what we call "fresh eyes"—noticing what's being discussed in the conversation (topic, data, and language used) and the people having the conversation (body language). This level is useful when multiple perspectives are being considered and differing points of view are being put forward. The coach stays open and non-judgmental, not engaging in a battle of ideas but instead listening and asking questions with an open mind.

Level 2 listening tips:

1. Count to four before responding to the other person.

2. Orient to accept 100-percent nonjudgmentally what the person is saying; open your mind.

3. Focus strongly on what the person is saying; wait with anticipation and genuine curiosity.

4. Give up on your idea; let it go.

5. Lean in and change your posture to show you're listening intently.

6. Nod and use other gestures to indicate you want them to continue talking.

7. Respond with: "And what else?" to what the other person says; evoke more depth.

Level 3 – When Clients Need to Feel Felt

Level 3 – Empathetic: This type of listening is focused on emotions, compassion, and empathy for the client. The aim is to have the client feel "felt." In other words, the client senses that you empathize with their situation and how they feel. This opens their heart and makes it safe for them to be vulnerable and honest. When you move into listening at this level, it invites the client to do the same and is a prerequisite for the conversation to move from debate to dialogue. If you open up, the client will follow; if you pretend to be open, the client will know your truth and respond by shutting down. The result is a "fake" open conversation with both parties pleasantly smiling but inwardly holding back.

A key factor in listening at this level for the agile coach is not trying to "fix" the client or give answers but remaining open and simply "holding the space" for the emotional conversation. Level-3 listening is not a comfortable place for most of the expert agile coaches I've encountered. In fact, it is a scary place for most experts who are used to dealing in facts, figures, and processes relating to agile. But responsive agile coaches learn how to go to level 3, work with people's emotions, and deeply listen. The best way to learn this is to practice.

When at this level, the main job of the coach is to sense what's emerging; usually emotions are the first sign of agreement to move forward and implement new agile ways of working. So don't ignore emotions; look for them and work with them as a means to help move the client forward in their adoption of agile.

Level 3 listening tips:

1. Orient to deeply caring for the person talking; feel for them and their situation.

2. Don't assess or judge their emotions. Definitely don't make a joke. No pity either.

3. Keep yourself calm and in control if emotions arise; often, your relaxed silence is enough to move the conversation along.

4. You're not a therapist, so don't act like one or try to fix the client.

5. Don't try to change the subject to avoid the emotions; hold the space.

6. When the timing is right, move the conversation forward towards action by asking: "What can we do to move forward?" or "What are these emotions telling us to do?"

Level 4 – When Everyone Needs to Reconnect to Purpose

Level 4 – Generative: This type of listening is a special skill and requires a well-developed ability to maintain an open mind and heart, ask the right questions, and then Await and let silence do the work. It's called generative listening, as it aims to bring about collective WILL (purpose) and a realization that change and a better way (of working) are possible. Although you may not spend a lot of time at this level right now (maybe no time at all), a responsive agile coach will spend more of their time here as they learn to Co-create new ways of working with their clients as opposed to downloading their opinions onto them (level 1).

A key indicator that you are listening at this level is that the conversation slows down; there are more pauses and silences where the client considers the questions they're being asked. At this level, the coach is waiting for signs on how to move into a better way of working with agile.

:

Level 4 listening tips:

1. Although you may want to fill the silence with conversation, do not.

2. When ideas start to flow, help them along, but be careful to not bring too much of your opinion into the conversation; listen for what is emerging in the client, not what is emerging in your mind.

3. Use all your senses and intuition when listening at level 4; as you practice this, you'll notice more and more.

4. If you notice something—posture change, a deep breath, or some other signal that something may have shifted in the client—offer it into the conversation without attaching your thoughts to it.

5. Continually orient your mindset to serve, saying to yourself, *How can I help the client move forward?* Just hold this mindset; do not allow yourself to generate thoughts or to provide solutions.

6. Maintain the right posture as you listen at level 4; try to maintain an upright and open posture that signals to the client that you are awaiting with curiosity for their next sentence.

How to Use Listening

The four levels listening model aligns with the Open and Hold move of the Responsive Agile Coaching model.

Practicing paying close attention to another person as they are talking is hard. The voice in our head does not shut-up, even for a second. So, part of adopting listening as a practice is non-judgmentally putting aside most of your inner conversation with yourself as you conduct an external one with the client; this is at the heart of the deeper levels of listening. Focus on the client and use question prompts to help you navigate your agile coaching conversations as opposed to preparing what you will say next while trying to listen to the client.

I know of no better way to move into levels 2 and 3 of listening than to orient your intent to totally serving the client's interests first and the organization's second. Once you get your intent set correctly, the client starts to notice (even if only intuitively), and this deepens the conversation; it's then up to you to ensure you "hold the space."

Chapter Summary

After questions, listening is the most important practice an agile coach must master.

* There are four levels of listening in the Responsive Agile Coaching model: downloading, factual, empathetic, and generative. These descriptors are drawn from the work of the Presencing Institute and are part of the Theory U body of knowledge.

* Downloading listening should be minimized, even if the agile coach is utilizing the Tell or Show move. Agile coaches should always be listening for signs that the client is ready to follow the down pathway; hence, they should listen at level 2 wherever possible.

* Levels 2 and 3 listening should be how the responsive agile coach listens as their default.

* Level 4 generative listening is often required for the deeper open WILL type coaching conversations. This level requires extensive practice in order for the coach to become proficient.

CHAPTER 16.

KEY PRACTICE – MINDFULNESS

Mindfulness: What It Is and Why It's Important?

"If awareness never reaches beyond superficial events and current circumstances, actions will be reactions."
— From *Presence*, a book by Peter Senge

Agile coaches are always making choices as they progress through a conversation with a client. *Should I tell or show them what to do? Should I listen or talk? Should I open up the conversation or close it down and move on?* The list goes on. So how does an agile coach know what is the right thing to do in the moment? Intuition plays a part, knowledge plays a part, knowing from learned experience is crucial, but mindfulness is a key capability that can be "activated" to help the coach make purposeful, considered decisions. Mindfulness allows the coach to resist deferring to their habits—the coach's known, safe responses—and allows them to explore new options *with* the client.

www.mindfulness.org gives us this definition:

> *"The basic human ability to be fully present, aware of where we are and what we're doing, and not overly reactive or overwhelmed by what's going on around us."*

Agile coaches should strive to be present for their clients, manage themselves, and respond to the cues from the situation so as to best serve the client. From the above definition, I'm hoping you can see that mindfulness has great potential to help agile coaches do their jobs.

Mindfulness is a universally accepted way to become a calmer, more grounded, less stressed, kind person. Who doesn't want that?

In a recent *Strategy & Business* article, "The Neuroscience of Leadership," brain scientists Jeffrey Schwartz and David Rock proposed:

> *"Organizations could marshal mindful attention to create organizational change. They could do this over time by putting in place regular routines in which people would watch the patterns of their thoughts and feelings as they worked and thus develop greater self-awareness."* [2]

Agile coaches, as leaders in the adoption of better ways to work, have a role in showing the way on the use of mindfulness as a means to create behavioral change. The question is, if mindfulness is so great, why doesn't everyone develop it as a capability? And why do I need to explain how good it is and "convince" you to consider it as part of your agile coaching practice?

The reason is simple; the benefits of a mindfulness practice can take time. There's a perceived delay between doing mindfulness exercises and the benefit that results or is experienced. Also, the benefits are somewhat indirect; it's not like when you learn how to hit a tennis ball—practicing for hours; slowly but surely experiencing improvement as you hit the ball with more accuracy and power. You may even nail one shot to the corner of the court and experience a moment where you do the perfect shot that one time. When you invest in mindfulness exercises or training, it usually does not work like that. You may undertake exercises for a few weeks and feel a little more relaxed while you do it, but often the effects are cumulative and take time. In an age of instant gratification, mindfulness just takes too long for people to see the benefit from doing the practices. And when the benefit comes, it's usually subtle at first and then, over time, leads to breakthrough moments of deep personal insight.

For me, mindfulness has been the key to being a better person while also enabling me to take on more senior roles as an agile coach. Without mindfulness I'd still be telling everyone who would listen that I have all the answers and that I should be listened to. Now I listen more, observe, and pause before offering my opinion and am more curious about the root cause of an issue than I am about quick, tactical process fixes. Mindfulness levels are a critical determinant to you becoming better at agile coaching. If you have trouble accepting yourself or others non-judgmentally and find it hard to adopt a non-expert mind and put aside your opinion and ego when required, then mindfulness is going to dramatically improve your coaching performance.

Often coaching moments (opportunities) are fleeting and need to be acted on immediately. This is what coaching "in the moment" means; it's an expected skill for an agile coach, and mindfulness is the key to executing it because it brings you back to the present (which is where the action is!).

When a coach is mindful, they are better equipped to Sense then Respond as they scan the environment for opportunities to coach. Mindful agile coaches can suspend their own thoughts and judgements. They keep their opinions out of conversations as they Open and Hold the space for conversations with clients. By doing this they give the client space to let come new ways to think and act; this is especially important for level 2 – 4 conversations.

Without mindfulness the coach doesn't even notice they are falling into old reactive habits of giving advice and telling the client when all the client requires from the coach is to be heard. The missing capability for the senior agile coaches I described earlier was their inability to mindfully choose instead of reactively being the expert.

Mindfulness Helps You to Make Meaning

As I became more self-aware, I was able to better *respond* to challenging situations instead of reacting; this was a meaningful experience for me. I'd like to share a recent piece of research that supports the idea that agile coaches can find meaning in their work by increasing their levels of mindfulness.

If you consider doctors working in hospitals, their job is to relieve suffering of patients. Agile coaches have similar aspirations to relieve workplace dysfunction that causes employees to have a poor experience of work. In a study titled "Enhancing Meaning in Work, A Prescription for Preventing Physician Burnout and Promoting Patient-Centered Care," Tait D. Shanafelt, MD investigated how mindfulness training can bring meaning into the work lives of doctors.

The findings of this study were remarkable in that a mere 52 hours of mindfulness exercises had a lasting effect 15 months later on a doctor's ability to make decisions that created more meaning at work. Here's a quote from the paper that sums it up nicely:

> *"Participants had large increases in mindfulness skills and orientation that were immediately detectable and were sustained for up to 15 months. The physicians also had large, durable improvements in burnout, mood disturbance, and empathy. These changes correlated with the improvements in mindfulness, suggesting that enhancing physicians' attention to their own experience not only increases their orientation toward patients but also reduces physician distress."* [3]

Another paper titled "Career Fit and Burnout Among Academic Faculty," written by the same author and his colleagues, investigated how much meaningful work was required to boost a worker's job satisfaction to adequate levels. Their research findings indicate that about one day per week of meaningful activity at work is enough to sustain you through the boring administrative activities we all sometimes have to do as part of our role. These meaningful activities do not have to occur on a daily basis but can be distributed throughout the week. [4]

My experience supports this; if I can do enough meaningful work within a role, I'll be happy and satisfied, even if I have to undertake administrative or menial work the majority of the time. But if my ability to "make" meaning is taken from me, then I start to assess if this role is right for me. As agile coaches we are fortunate, as we (should) have ample opportunity to have meaningful conversations as we help others learn and grow through our coaching work. The Responsive Agile Coaching model is a meaning-making model to conduct agile coaching conversations, and mindfulness is a doorway to this meaning. If you learn how to use it correctly, you will have no trouble generating moments of meaning throughout your day and week; you just need to adopt it as a practice. One of the best ways to implement "moments of meaning" into your coaching is through mindfulness exercises.

Mindfulness Exercises

It is beyond the scope of this book to outline in detail how an agile coach could develop a mindfulness practice, so I will limit this section to a short guide on key aspects to consider.

Mindfulness is not a special thing; it is always available. We just need to pay attention. If, for a moment, we can stop rehashing the past or rehearsing the future, we will arrive at the present moment, and if we pay attention, we will be mindful of what is happening.

Let's do a short mindfulness practice to help you get the basics.

Below is a three-minute routine. You'll realize it seems simple; that's because it is. Mindfulness is like a lot of practices—simple to learn, difficult to master. Remember, it is supposed to be practiced, so it will feel strange if you've never done anything like this before:

Mindfulness Exercise

1. Turn off your phone notifications and any other devices; remove all distractions.

2. Set a timer with a gentle sounding chime for three minutes.

3. Sit up straight in your chair. It's best if it is a firm seat.

4. Imagine a string is pulling the back of your head upward. Your chin should be slightly tucked in, and your mouth should be closed.

5. Place your hands on your thighs.

6. Close your eyes or just lower your eyelids.

7. Breathe from your belly.

8. Say to yourself as you follow your breath going in and out: *Breathing in, breathing out, deep, slow, calm, relaxed.* Keep repeating this as you breathe for three minutes.

9. Your mind will wander; guaranteed. When it does, notice and come back to your breath. This is the practice! Coming back to where you are. Also, notice your posture; come back to sitting up straight if you tilt or lean.

10. Repeat for three minutes (or longer if at home; up to 20 minutes is good to start with).

11. When the timer rings, stop and reflect. How do you feel? What did you notice before, during, and after? Maybe write your reflections down in a journal.

If you have never done anything like this before, it seems very far removed from being a responsive agile coach. You just want to be an expert on agile, I get it, but there will come a day when that is not enough, and you will need the capability to mindfully put aside your agile expertise. I cannot put this more plainly; start practicing now so you build your mindfulness into your coaching from the start. Then, as your expert knowledge builds, you will also be developing the ability to respond and follow a conversation pathway that best serves the client.

The above practice example is one method; there are many, but they all have the same principles of returning your attention to the present moment.

It is the noticing and returning that is the practice.

Here are some suggestions on how to plan mindfulness into your day. I usually recommend trying at least one of three *means* to bring mindfulness into your life:

1. **Mind** – working with your thoughts

   This involves some form of observing your thoughts and accepting them without judgement and is usually associated with meditation, like what I described in the above exercise.

2. **Heart** – working with your emotions/feelings

   This involves compassion or gratitude activities and is usually integrated with meditation but can be done as a journaling exercise where you write to give thanks for what is in your life.

3. **Body** – working with your sensations/posture

   Meditation has a physical aspect, but yoga or mindful walking takes this a step further to integrate the body into the present moment. Mindfully checking your posture at work engages the body too.

By practicing returning back to the present moment, you are improving your ability to choose, but the other thing this enables is it allows you to reorient yourself to your intent to serve the client. In other words, it helps you to remind yourself why you are here and what you are supposed to be paying attention to.

In developing your mindfulness it's important to take your own tendencies into consideration. If you are a very logical thinker, you may be drawn to meditation to calm your mind; whereas if you are a feeler type of person, then the heart practices may interest you. Irrespective, I would encourage you to get your posture right when coaching; it is a core practice that centers you, especially under pressure or in stressful situations. An upright spine and the ability to breathe deeply from your belly are things you can try right away, today. Do it and notice how it brings your attention back and helps you focus.

Creating Your Mindfulness Practice

When I'm mentoring coaches, I suggest they practice mindfulness in any one of three ways or "methods." Each can be done independently or can be used in combination; it depends on what works for the individual coach, their lifestyle, and preferences. The three *methods* to implement mindfulness into your day are:

- **Formal** practice: usually conducted outside of the workplace, at home, at a scheduled time.

- **Informal** practice: via "pauses" in your routine throughout the day, scheduled or unscheduled.

- **Incidental** practice: as part of your activity; mindfulness as you work/live; usually using a trigger event or activity.

I suggest you make yourself a mindfulness plan that combines one or multiple "means" from the previous section with one or multiple "methods" listed above and just start. This involves investing time and effort so as to build you capability to be mindful. For example, here is a proposed plan that invests between 20 and 42 minutes per day in developing mindfulness:

- 6:00 a.m.: 10- to 20-minute silent meditation.

- Start every phone call with an awareness check-in to sit up straight with upright posture.

- During the course of the day, three to four 2-minute mindful breathing routine practices.

- 9.30 p.m.: Gratitude journaling to give thanks for blessings in your life; five to ten minutes.

This is only a short guide, but I strongly recommend you buy a few books in this topic. I have listed some recommendations at the end of this part of the book.

Let's now examine another use for mindfulness—changing your habits.

Chapter Summary

- Mindfulness has many benefits for us as people but also enables agile coaches to accelerate their ability to be more responsive.

- The means by which you can bring mindfulness into your life include: mind (thoughts), body (posture and sensations), or heart (feelings and empathy) practices.

- The method by which you can bring mindfulness into your life includes formal practice at home, informal practice at work, and incidental practices throughout the day.

- Creating a mindfulness plan and implementing it now will support you to build responsiveness into your coaching as your career progresses.

CHAPTER 17.

KEY PRACTICE – HABIT MANAGEMENT

Agile Coaching Habits

Responsive agile coaches have the ability to choose the right move depending on what best serves the client and the circumstances. Masterful coaches—once they've become skilled in executing all the moves I've mentioned—can dance between the pathways in real time, taking the conversation down and then across as required. My experience has taught me that to develop this level of responsiveness, agile coaches need to change some old habits and learn some new ones.

Habits are a very important aspect of agile coaching. A habit is defined as:

"A settled or regular tendency or practice, especially one that is hard to give up."

As I mentioned at the start of the book, many expert agile coaches have lost their ability to think like a beginner; they've established a habit of automatically giving advice (Tell or Show). Whereas beginner agile coaches need to be aware of the new habits they need to become great agile coaches. So, habits are a big deal for agile coaches; in the remainder of this chapter, I'll spend some time outlining just how habits work and how they impact your ability to responsively coach.

The Structure of a Habit

Agile coaching conversations with clients are personal; your habits, traits, and personality come into play as you conduct a conversation. To coach, you need to have high levels of awareness of your habits and how they affect you as you talk with others. A great agile coach knows which of their habits are serving the client and which are not during coaching conversations. Once you see how habits work, you can then alter yours to improve your coaching. This is essentially how to develop into a responsive agile coach—by changing your habitual reactions as you talk to clients. Sounds simple, but it takes a lifetime to master. Here is a picture to explain the elements of a habit; I'll explain this in the following sections.

Cues

A cue signals to your habit to start running; it kicks off a behavioral routine, automatic reaction, process, or behavior. Habits aim to save us (specifically our brain's) energy by providing shortcuts to solutions without us having to think. Most of the time they serve us and produce the reward we're seeking, but sometimes they are not useful.

A large part of being a responsive coach is keeping your opinions, ideas, and judgement out of a conversation to allow the client to safely share what's on their mind. By safely I mean without you judging, assessing, or offering alternatives to what they have to say about the problem they're facing. One of the reasons I wrote this book was because I observed a consistent habit from senior agile coaches; let's call it the "expert" habit. This habit is not just an agile coaching challenge; it is a very human trait to respond to someone's problem with what you think the solution is. But as agile coaches we need to resist the urge (craving, in habit terminology) to offer our advice, solutions, experience, ideas, or opinions when it does not help the client.

Most coaches don't know they have the expert habit; how about you? When you hear a big juicy problem a client is facing and you've solved it previously, what's your immediate reaction? I'll provide more guidance on how to manage your reaction to a cue like this later. Right now, I just want you to understand that cues exist and that you may not be noticing that cues have you running a habitual routine, which may or may not serve your clients.

Routine

As mentioned in the previous section, a routine is like a program you run when it's activated (cued). Routines run mostly on autopilot; that's why it is part of a habit—remember, it saves energy; you don't have to think. Usually habitual routines are behaviors, but they can also be thoughts, stories you tell yourself, and/or physical responses. Sometimes when a person's cue is triggered, they have a reaction in their body. Remember a time when you overheard someone asking another person a question you knew the answer to, and you immediately jumped into the conversation to provide an answer; that was a cue that was triggered by something that affected you. It ran the routine "PROVIDE SOLUTION," for which you were (probably) rewarded with a thank you from those you provided the information to.

As a coach you need to be able to change which routine you run in response to the cues that signal it is time for you to coach (do your job).

Craving

So, how is it that these habits become so engrained in us? The answer is that it satisfies a craving, or a *"powerful desire to have something."* Cravings are the engine house of a habit; they give the habit energy and power. Without a craving, a habit won't form. Marketing and sales professionals have used cravings as a means to get people to buy things that have no proven efficacy or are unhealthy for the consumer. Think of alcohol and tobacco but also standard consumer goods like toothpaste and shampoo. For example, the foaming properties of shampoo and toothpaste have no value to the consumer, but they create a craving due to the aesthetic experience when the products are used. In fact, the tingling of toothpaste has been identified by neuroscientists as a key driver of the adoption of toothpaste post-world World War II. The tingling adds nothing to help clean teeth, but people don't consider the product to be doing its job unless there is a tingling feeling when brushing.

Agile coaches in my experience have been recognized and rewarded for being experts by providing the answers to agile implementation problems. This has created an industry-wide craving for being THE expert together with being right and being heard. Some of the most counter-productive agile coaching habits have also included the craving to be in control. For a moment, imagine an agile coach who craves being right, being heard, and being in control; it might almost make you laugh, but it is no joke because I've seen many agile coaches who have these cravings and associated habits. The natural extension of this thinking leads to "whoever has the most agile knowledge is the best agile coach." I refute this, of course, and argue that although agile coaches should have knowledge of agile (duh!), the expert-habit is responsible for a lack of responsiveness in many senior agile coaches. This craving to be the expert runs against their ability to be a responsive agile coach because every time their answer is not accepted by the client, they end up in a debate, unable to move the conversation into dialogue; they get stuck. This points to the need for unlearning and modification of existing habits in many senior agile coaches (more on this in the next chapter).

Your Personality and Social Style

As agile coaches we need to be more aware than the average professional of how our personalities impact our work. Your personality has a significant effect on which habits you form. Recent research by Benjamin Chapman and Lewis Goldberg published in *Personality and Individual Differences* examined a wide set (400) of mundane, incidental, or "everyday" behavioral acts (habits) and found significant statistical associations with personality.[5] For example, people scoring low on "Conscientiousness" are prone to procrastination. There is also one example that is quite amusing, where high "Agreeableness" is correlated with singing in the shower. In short, your personality and behavioral habits are strongly correlated.

As coaches we do not have the luxury of letting our habits run our routines unchecked during our conversations with clients. Coaches, like all people, regulate their habits through different areas in the brain. It is these often competing voices in our head that, after a difficult day of work, argue the merits of "eating the donut or the apple"; one automatic routine is seeking emotional and sensory pleasure (by eating a donut), while the other choice you could make (instead of the habit's routine) is the logical, healthy choice (eat the apple). I won't go into the brain science now, but when we're delivering agile coaching, these same voices are at play. Habitual reactions are strongly influencing the internal conversation we have with ourselves: *Do I tell them what I know, or should I let the client discover the answer for himself/herself?*

The challenge for agile coaches is that sometimes our personality and associated habits are so ingrained and produce behavior so quickly once triggered that we do not even know we are in a moment where we have a choice. Coaches may have developed such low awareness of these habits that it could be compared to a fish in water; the fish does not know what water is because it is immersed in it.

Different personalities have different needs in social situations. What people "crave" when they talk and interact with other people varies. One way to present how agile coaches interact with clients is described as their "Social Style." Research has shown this to have explanatory power when attempting to identify how different people perceive a social interaction (such as during an agile coaching conversation).[6] The social styles model helps agile coaches understand what they and their clients want from conversations. In the table below I've paraphrased some of the research points on the different styles; it shows what each style is seeking out of a social interaction. The point is that to be a responsive agile coach, you must be able to control whatever social needs/cravings you have when in a client conversation. Your needs must be put aside in service of what the client's needs are, even if it goes against your personality or social style.

Perfectionist - need to be right	**Controller** - need to be the boss
Team player - need to be accepted	**Attention seeker** - need to be heard

If we apply this model to conducting an agile coaching conversation, you'll start to see just why it can be so hard to deliver responsive agile coaching. For example, imagine if you have a strong need (a craving even) to be heard because you're an "attention seeker." As a coach it is not your job to be the center of attention; you're supposed to be putting your client's needs first. In this example, your social style wants the conversation to be centered on your needs and what you've got to say. Of course, this is not helpful, as the conversation should be about the client feeling heard so as to help them work through their challenges in adopting agile. The same goes for the other personality types: controllers will need to let go; perfectionists need to let the client work through ambiguity at their own pace.

So, whatever any personality test describes you as, it does not matter; as a responsive agile coach, your challenge is to develop the ability to put aside your personality's needs and what you crave from social interactions (i.e., a coaching conversation) and stay open and flexible in service of the client.

The Reward from Agile Coaching

The usual reward for an agile coach is solving the client's agile adoption problem. If an agile coach can look back at a system of work they have been coaching and observe behavioral change and a mindset shift in the people working in the system, then they have their reward for a job well done. Additionally, if the system is self-learning and can continuously improve without the need for the coach to be present, then the coach has embedded the way of working.

The above is one reward agile coaches receive; there are many more, such as fulfilment for helping others, making a difference, or being part of something important and bigger than oneself. The point is that none of these are "bad" or "good"; it is the habitual routines we run to get our rewards that are the focus when attempting to alter a habit. How do you alter a habit? You *unlearn* parts of it. We will go into detail on this concept in the next chapter.

Chapter Summary

♦ Managing your habits and the effect of your social style on how you coach starts by having awareness; so, start paying attention to what you do habitually and your personality traits.

♦ Your habits and personality have been shown to be closely related. Be aware of your personality and the different routines you are running once a habit is triggered by its cue.

♦ The "expert" habit is a big issue in agile coaching; so, be aware of your agile expertness playing too big of a role in your coaching. Learn to be a non-expert when appropriate.

CHAPTER 18.

KEY PRACTICE – UNLEARNING

I f you attain all the agile knowledge and have demonstrated your skills in the practices of agile with support from a mentor and persisted for a few years, you will most likely get to your goal of delivering high-quality agile coaching but will probably not be a responsive agile coach. "What? Why?" I hear you ask. Responsive agile coaches do not just learn new capabilities; they unlearn old habits. Unlearning is not a new phenomenon, but it has been popularized recently with books on the subject and is seen as a critical tool when aiming for mindset shifts in the workforce during an agile transformation. The concept of unlearning together with the related fields of neuroscience and behavioral psychology provide coaches with important tools to accelerate their career development; hence, I see it as a key practice. So, what exactly do I mean when I refer to unlearning unhelpful habits? Well, it's not about stopping your habits; it's about modifying them.

Your habitual reactions are triggered by cues—strong behavioral patterns that are (almost) impossible to remove—but the overall habit can be changed, altered. Let me explain. In the picture below, I've highlighted the routine element of how habits work.

We've already covered habits in the previous chapter, but I want to focus on one specific aspect that is central to helping you unlearn—the routines you run.

In the book, *The Power of Habit*, Charles Duhigg concluded that habits are so powerful that we shouldn't try to get rid of them but instead modify them. He goes on to say that the cue for a habit and the reward for following a habitual behavior are very difficult to change, whereas the routine in the middle is most easily modified. He suggests that's where we should focus (when unlearning).[7]

For example, when you are asked a question like, "Should the product owner always attend the retrospective?" your habitual reaction may be to provide your opinion/answer so as to demonstrate your expertise, receive the reward of "client satisfaction," and fulfil your craving for "being right." But what if giving your answer to the question is not the best way to serve the client? What if this question is best answered through a level-3 agile coaching conversation?

This is where a responsive agile coach chooses an alternative move (to Telling or Showing the client) by running a different routine within the same habit that results in the same reward. In this example, an agile coach would withstand the temptation to give in to their craving "to be right" and instead attain the same reward by conducting a deeper coaching conversation (Open and Hold move).

We can use this same approach for all our unhelpful habits—modifying the routines that don't serve us or our clients. Below are the habits I see agile coaches need to change and unlearn if they want to deliver responsive agile coaching. You may not have these habits yet; if so, take note of them anyway so that you can keep an eye on yourself and your behavior as you progress through your career.

Unlearning Opportunity #1 – "I Am the Expert" Reaction

This first habit is central to becoming a responsive agile coach and needs to be unlearned if you want to excel in more senior roles.

Unlearn your expert reaction when asked to help solve agile problems.

As I have made clear previously, a responsive agile coach's first action to being asked an agile question is to stop, suspend their expertise, and sense the environment to consider what will best serve the client. To do this, an agile expert needs to unlearn the habitual reaction of acting as an expert.

I'm sure you've experienced that little dopamine hit you get when you are recognized as the person who solved the problem by way of delivering information or practical advice. It feels good, right? Of course, it does; who doesn't like being right and solve someone's problem?

I often speak to agile coaches about their motivations; it is consistent that they enjoy and achieve a sense of purpose from getting this little reward. Please do not think I am against us getting rewarded for having the right answer to client's questions—it's very important—BUT my observations tell me this has created such a strong expert habit that coaches have lost their ability to respond. Let me take you through two more unlearning opportunities, then I'll provide you tips on how to modify unhelpful habits utilizing an unlearning method.

Unlearning Opportunity #2 – Problem-Solving Reaction

The agile coach who believes they always have the solution to the client problem is quick to start solving; it is a reaction, not a response.

The routine an agile coach runs if they have this habit is to see a problem and immediately fill their mind with the answer and/or voice their answer straight into the conversation. Both are not helpful, but the latter is the most problematic, as it interrupts the conversation flow and could trigger the client to start a debate with the coach.

The unlearning opportunity here is for the coach to recognize they are about to run their habitual routine of providing a solution, pause, and consider if downloading their answer (Tell or Show) is going to help the client or if the Open and Hold move would better serve the situation. The trigger is the same "client problem," and the reward is the same "problem solved," but the routine is changed to "coach Opens and Holds" instead of the coach's habitual routine of "Tell or Show" the client the answer. Of course, if the appropriate answer is to simply Tell the client what to do and the coach does so responsively, then great; this is a good outcome.

Unlearning Opportunity #3 – Emotion-Avoiding Reaction

In Chapter 9 I spent some time discussing how an agile coach has the job of moving conversations from debate to dialogue by opening their heart. To do this, coaches will be working with emotions. To avoid emotions is like an agile coach saying, "I don't want to work with humans," seeing the world as a process to be optimized and dismissing what drives most human behavior.

It is hard to believe that many agile coaches I work with struggle to introduce their client's emotions into a conversation. The habits they've formed default to logic, process, and tooling as solutions to agile problems. But fundamentally, all agile coaching problems are about people, and every person's behavior is strongly influenced by their emotions.

By practicing mindfulness, an agile coach will become more self-aware with regards to their own emotional state and how their clients *feel* about a situation. By increasing your level of awareness regarding emotions, you will be able to spot when you are starting to run a habitual routine that aims to avoid an emotional conversation.

The first signal that emotions are entering a coaching conversation could either be your feelings or those of your client. Being on the lookout for changes to your internal state or signs that your client is becoming emotional are both important skills for agile coaches. Without this emotional detection skill, you miss the signals that the client is sending, you don't serve the client's need, and the conversation remains superficial. Coaches with this habit usually end up downloading their ideas, solutions, or answers onto the client, ignoring the signals (from the client) that are "requesting" emotions be brought into the conversation. The agile coach walks away thinking they've done a great job, they've got *their* reward, but the client leaves unsatisfied.

An Approach to Unlearning

The practice of unlearning is central to becoming a responsive agile coach. In order to best serve your clients, it's important to continuously be on the lookout for signs that you are forming unhelpful habits. Once you suspect an unlearning opportunity, you can then put the practice I'm about to show you in place, or something similar. Here's the step-by-step approach I use to unlearn and help others do the same:

1. **Describe the cue that triggers**: The first step to unlearning a habit is to spot the cue that triggers (starts) the unhelpful routine to run. The more precise and detailed your description of the trigger, the higher the chance of you noticing and being able to substitute an alternate routine (respond and not react). It will be important to write down when, where, who, and other information on yourself that relates to the cue and trigger.

2. **Design an alternate routine** to experiment with what will be substituted for the unhelpful one. For example, when someone asks you an agile question, instead of reacting quickly with an answer to demonstrate your knowledge, you will pause, take a breath, and consider the intent of the question and the person for three to five seconds. The usual script when designing a habit experiment is to write it using this format:

   > When____<<*insert cue here*>>____ happens,
   > I will ____<<*insert new routine here*>>____,
   > instead of____<<*insert old routine here*>>____,
   > so that____<<*insert benefit/reward here*>> ____.

3. **Set your intent to practice** during the following days and weeks. Go into your day knowing this is a live experiment and focus on where there may be opportunities to practice (run your experiment). Doing this will increase the chance of you noticing your cues, enabling you to run alternate routines. Construct your unlearning experiment to run over a set period of time (a timebox).

4. **Recognize, observe, and monitor:** cognitive behavioral therapy (CBT) utilizes this step in the form of a reflective journal to help patients assess their negative thoughts and emotions; this psychological technique can also be applied to your unlearning practice. Unlike in CBT where the patient is aiming to use their journaling to challenge false beliefs, we're using this as an opportunity to challenge our unhelpful routines and substitute alternate ones. Maintain a journal and record your daily experiments; take notes on your thoughts and insights. Reflect and then re-plan your next set of experiments. Use this journal to record outcomes as you test your hypothesis regarding your habits. Just by noticing your behavior you are already changing it for the better; that's why CBT is so powerful.

5. **Go public and get support.** Never try to change a habit without help from those around you. To go it alone only leads you to having internal struggles; share your goals with people you feel you can be a little vulnerable and open with. Seek feedback and ask for help, especially in recognizing and monitoring your efforts to notice cues and routines. Also, talk to your mentor and peers, who I recommend you show your journal to and work with to help design experiments.

6. **Review after a timebox.** After the timebox is finished, assess the insights and results from your experiment. If the data (facts) and how you feel indicate that you have effectively embedded the new routine into your old habit, then you may close the experiment; if not, design a new

one. Your journal will have both insights and feelings as well as the required data to help you assess what to do.

It is important to not run too many unlearning experiments at the same time. I usually advise coaches I'm mentoring to work on a maximum of two habits at once. By limiting your experiments in progress to two, it allows you to deepen your insights and speeds up the unlearning process.

Now would be a good time to pause reading and design some experiments for yourself. Use the unlearning opportunities I've provided as a start and then add your own. Talk to peers or those close to you who could reveal additional habits that the people around you find unhelpful. This practice can be used in any area of your life and is not just for agile coaching.

Chapter Summary

- Unlearning simply refers to changing the habitual and often reactive routines we run that are triggered by cues as we go about our lives.

- There are three opportunities where agile coaches can unlearn unhelpful behaviors: being a reactive expert, reactively providing solutions, and avoiding emotional conversations.

- It is recommended that agile coaches develop their practice in unlearning using the template provided.

CHAPTER 19.

KEY PRACTICE – EVOKING PRESENCE

What Is Presence, and Why Is It Important?

Being mindful is in your control, and for coaches it is used as a means to evoke presence during client conversations. Presence is a pre-condition to co-creating new agile ways of working; it's a state that is evoked when an agile coach is able to "hold the space" for the conversation.

You know presence exists because we've all experienced moments when suddenly the possibilities open up and you see "the greater whole" that is around the issue or problem you have been dealing with. You simultaneously see both the tree and the forest and realize there is a way forward. Some people call it a "reframe" or an "ah-ha!" moment where your view on something changes and you see things from a different perspective. Doug Silsby was one of the world leaders on how coaches work with presence, he defined presence as:

> *"A state of awareness, in the moment, characterized by the felt experience of timelessness, connectedness, and a larger truth."*

This idea of a "larger truth" is important for us as agile coaches, as it represents the client seeing how the bigger picture relates to their specific personal situation. The agile coach's job is to help the client see this bigger picture or larger truth and then work with us to plot a way forward to better ways of working.

If you are a logic-driven person, you might struggle with this explanation of presence and be tempted to dismiss this whole chapter and skip to the process of delivering agile coaching. Stay with me; otherwise, you'll miss a key element of how the Responsive Agile Coaching model works.

Often clients experience presence when they have breakthrough moments. You too will have had these moments; sometimes they are deep and profound; other times, just an interesting, new perspective emerges in the moment. Presence is often referred to as a "felt experience" and is most apparent during the Await then Co-create move in the Responsive Agile Coaching model.

Presence is often discussed as a spiritual concept, but this is just coincidence. It is because deep insights come from the stillness and silence of meditation, prayer, yoga, or other activities related to religious practice. But presence is frequently evoked in the workplace too; consider the last time you were in a workshop and suddenly people started to click, the ideas flowed, egos disappeared, and everyone was energized around a common purpose. We all know what it's like when we don't have presence in meetings too, I'm sure.

In agile coaching, presence is a desirable condition during deeper conversations that bring about change in people's perspectives on how their role fits into the wider system of work. The person or team being coached will "let go" of how they saw their old way of working and "let come" the new, co-created way of working. It is for this reason that presence-based agile coaching is one of the main prerequisites for behavioral change to embed; it enables individuals and teams to see this larger truth of how they can fit into the bigger picture as the organization moves to an agile way of working. The people you're coaching stop doing agile as a process and start being agile; they internalize the change as a result of you facilitating deep (open WILL) conversations.

Presencing Reflection

Take a moment to remember a key event in your life where you had a breakthrough realization or a peak emotional experience. It could be when you proposed to your now wife/husband and were awaiting their response. It could be the moment you heard the news that you got a job you really wanted. For some it might be the moment you finally got to a personal or professional peak you'd been ascending towards for a long time and are taking a moment to bask in the achievement.

For me it's when I'm deeply talking to someone I'm mentoring; being profoundly interested in what they're about to say next; the anticipation of where the conversation could go.

Let's try a visualization now, as you're reading.

Sit up straight where you are, close your eyes, and take a deep breath from your lower stomach. Now, if you remember back to a scenario similar to the examples I described above, visualize in your mind what was happening, who was there, what was being said. How did you feel when it struck you (the insight or ah-ha!)?

Consider this for a moment; pause, close your eyes, and visualize the moment.

If you had to describe the atmosphere, "vibe," or mood in the room, what words would you use? It's hard, right? Interestingly, it isn't necessary to describe it in words because it was felt and experienced as a special moment where possibilities opened up and something shifted in you and/or in the group you were with. New things were possible, and some old things had been left behind. These moments have the potential to unlock significant amounts of change in the people you coach; break-throughs not incremental improvements; that's why as coaches we need to practice evoking presence.

Working with Presence

The conditions in which these realization moments occur can be contrived. In fact, it is an agile coach's job to set clients up to have these experiences of insight and realization. In all of the stories I've told so far in the book, there have been moments where silence has been used to allow for a moment to arise. It is in these moments of silence that the coach is evoking presence by awaiting. It provides space to "let come" what is being co-created in that moment. The coach does not push their opinion or ideas or solutions but simply "holds the space" for the client. The coach may offer some contributions as presence is arising in a conversation, but it is in the spirit of co-creation, not telling the client the answer.

How do you learn to do this? Let me keep this very simple. The coach pays full attention and has an attitude to serve those he/she is coaching AND does this with an open mind, heart, and will. The secret to evoking presence is to show up fully present, fully committed to helping, then observe without judgement or agenda, being still, deeply listening, and then awaiting to see what emerges from the silence. As ideas and insights start to present themselves, the coach then acts, asking questions that support the person or people they're coaching to find a path to adoption of better ways of working.

I gave you more specific guidance on how to do this in Chapters 9 and 10, but I would like you to understand that presence is real and is to be taken seriously if you are to deliver responsive agile coaching to clients. So, practice evoking it using the questions and listening practices I've provided you.

Chapter Summary

+ Presence is a state of awareness, in the moment, characterized by the felt experience of timelessness, connectedness, and a larger truth.

+ In agile coaching, this larger truth often refers to the client seeing the bigger picture around the problem they're facing as they adopt agile as a way to work.

+ Presence can be evoked through the use of the key practices outlined in this part of the book, especially mindfulness and listening.

+ Presence-based agile coaching conversations will significantly improve your ability to embed change.

References and Further Reading

1. Presencing Institute; www.presencing.org.

2. Jeffrey Schwartz and David Rock, "The Neuroscience of Leadership," *Strategy & Business*, (May 2006).

3. Tait D. Shanafelt MD et al, "Career fit and burnout among academic faculty," *JAMA Internal Medicine*, (May 2009): 990-995.

4. Tait D. Shanafelt MD, "Enhancing Meaning in Work. A Prescription for Preventing Physician Burnout and

Promoting Patient-Centered Care," *JAMA,* (September 2009): 1338-1340.

5. Benjamin P. Chapman and Lewis R. Goldberg, "Act frequency signatures of the Big Five," *Personality and Individual Differences* 116 (October 2017): 201-205.

6. William B. Snavely, "The impact of social style upon person perception in primary relationships," *Communication Quarterly,* (May 2009): 132-143.

7. Charles Duhigg, *The Power of Habit: Why We Do What We Do and How to Change,* (Random House, 2012).

8. Barry, O'Reilly, *Unlearn: Let Go of Past Success to Achieve Extraordinary Results,* (McGraw-Hill Education, 2018).

9. Michael Bungay Stainer, *Coaching Habit; Say Less, Ask More & Change the Way You Lead Forever,* (Box of Crayons, 2006).

10. Doug Silsbee, *The Mindful Coach: Seven Roles for Facilitating Leader Development, New and Revised Edition,* (John Wiley & Sons Inc, 2010).

11. Betty Sue Flowers, C. Otto Scharmer, Joseph Jaworski, Peter M. Senge, *Presence: Exploring Profound Change in People, Organizations and Society,* (John Murray Press, 2005).

12. Bob Stahl and Elisha Goldstein, *A Mindfulness-Based Stress Reduction Workbook,* (New Harbinger Publications Inc., 2010).

13. Go to www.responsiveagile.coach to learn with others who have read or are reading this book; you can also visit www.responsiveagilecoaching.com for up-to-date content, downloads, and templates.

PART V
A RESPONSIVE AGILE COACHING CAREER

Introduction

Before we get into the how of building a responsive agile coaching career, I want to ensure that you understand the development process for agile coaches. It's a journey, an adventure, that can be a transformative experience, especially if you truly want to become a responsive agile coach. This chapter is important, as it explicitly takes you through an example of the transformative development process to becoming proficient in responsive agile coaching. Being able to responsively coach in the moment is not like turning on a light switch; it is a medium to a long-term developmental undertaking. So, I want to spend a little time to help you understand what this means, then I'll tell you a real-life story of a typical career journey to proficiency.

To become truly masterful as an agile coach, you will focus on personal development more so than you would in other technical career paths. As a coach, you're working with people, their values and purposes; to do this, you need to be in touch with your own biases and the emotional "triggers" that make you react in unhelpful ways. It is a journey that involves deep change, hard work, persistence, courage, and a thirst for learning—learning not only new agile knowledge and skills but also about your own traits, personality, strengths, weaknesses, values, etc. And, of course, there's lots to unlearn too.

All of this is required so that you can serve your client. Responsive agile coaches ensure their attitudes and opinions don't get in the way of listening to what their client's needs are; this allows them to then help the client work toward new ways of working and being.

CHAPTER 20.

RESPONSIVE AGILE COACHING ACROSS A CAREER

What Does It Take to Deliver Responsive Agile Coaching?

To research this book, I've interviewed hundreds of coaches and asked them about their journeys and how they got to where they are. I'll expand on this in detail in subsequent chapters, but for now I want you to appreciate the significance of the journey you may wish to undertake.

It takes a blend of knowledge, experience, and a dedication to personal growth to develop the responsive capabilities outlined in this book. Part of the problem with defining great agile coaching is that it is difficult to explain what the journey to becoming great looks like. It is a rich and iterative learning experience that is impossible to capture in a bullet-point list, graph, or consultant model.

Some (not many) agile coaches are naturals; their personalities and traits make the role a good fit for them. These naturals don't have to totally transform themselves to become good coaches, but I would argue that to become great they still need to do considerable work on themselves. I want to take a minute and outline the type of agile coaching role types I've seen in the market; this will be useful as you consider your development goals as you read the following chapters.

Agile Coaching Role Types

As a typical career develops, the how you coach and who you coach of agile coaching changes. I want to quickly go through the types of roles you may encounter as you work to deliver agile coaching over the course of a career.

By aspiring to your next role or career step, you will have to challenge yourself and who you are and let go of some parts of yourself to make room for or "let come" new habits, values, and beliefs.

What I have not told you yet is what happens to you as you undertake the practices outlined in the practice guide chapter. You've probably figured it out by now, but to become a responsive agile coach is a transformative journey. Agile coaching shapes who you are because in order to conduct deep conversations with others, you need to grow as a person; that's why I think agile coaching roles are the coolest to have. Great agile coaches are great people; helping and serving others to be the best they can be.

So, progressing in your agile coaching career journey involves different responsive agile coaching conversations with different people at different levels in the organization. Let's have a look at some typical roles coaches progress through during their careers.

Agile Coaching – the Three Roles in a Career

I'd like to spend a little time demystifying and simplifying the types of agile coaching roles that exist. There is no set and agreed way to list all the types of roles in the market, so I'm going to generalize a bit and reduce all agile coaching roles down to three main types aligned to the size of the system of work being coached:

- ◆ Agile Coaching Small – a system of work involving 2 – 30 people

- Agile Coaching Medium – a system of work involving 31 – 300 people

- Agile Coaching Large – a system of work involving 301 – 1300 people

For systems of work any larger than 1300 people, I would argue you're probably not doing much coaching and most of your work is consulting or managing. I've worked at all the above levels as an agile practitioner (doer), agile coach (enabler) and agile consultant (problem solver). Each level is important and has its challenges and rewards. Agile coaches usually progress through their career from small through medium and on to large as a sequence, and I would argue this is the right way to go about it. Working in small systems of work is where you learn the basics and how to do them well before thinking about what it means to scale up your coaching practice into the bigger systems of work.

I want to spend a moment looking at each of the roles to help you understand a little more about what's involved at each size. You can then make a conscious choice about what your next career goal is; this will help you as we progress through the rest of the book.

The Start – Working with Yourself

Wait a minute; before we go off and discuss coaching roles, we need to make sure you understand the first person you need to coach is yourself—a system of one. I know this sounds silly, but I've worked with too many agile coaches for too long, and you wouldn't believe the number of times I have had to pull a coach aside who is facing a problem "out there" only to tell them their problem is "them." Most of our problems have a fair percentage that is about us (as coaches) and not the system we are coaching.

This is important to understand so that you continually assess your part in all the challenges you face as an agile coach. One way to monitor if you are taking enough personal responsibility is to keep track of how often you complain; coaches who whine a lot and are victims usually have more work to do on themselves. Always continue to work on who you are and how you affect the people and system of work around you. This always has to be in your awareness; once you have your own self in-hand (as much as one can), you then turn your attention to the system of work you are coaching or the next role you're aspiring to land.

To ensure you are always coaching yourself, my advice is to create and maintain a development plan that is considered as part of how you work. More on this later. Right now, let's consider each size coaching role, what each involves, and learn about the key aspects you need to consider in your career journey.

Agile Coaching Small

Never, ever, skip this role; don't jump straight to coaching in larger systems of work. If you do start your career coaching larger systems of work (like I did), make sure you come back and coach one to three teams for six months to a year (like I did).

Why am I making this point so strongly? So many coaches get obsessed about scaling agile. Anyone who knows anything about agile knows that it wasn't supposed to be scaled; it was designed for small- to medium-sized product organizations. My point is that although scaled agile is very real and is an important part of modern business, agile coaches need to deeply appreciate and have direct experience working with one to three teams and do agile well before thinking about larger systems of work.

The experience you'll get from maturing a team's agile practices and helping them deliver increments of value every sprint (or continuously) in a sustainable way is irreplaceable. Some of my fondest memories are of sitting next to developers and a customer to discuss a new feature—using conversations to ellicit the details of the need of the customer, then having it ready to ship next sprint and turning to the product owner, who nods, and it goes live.

My other favorite memory is working with a business team who were learning their way forward through a customer problem—testing, learning, and trialing a solution live and in real time to test assumptions as they fine-tuned a product design using insights gained from field tests. We shipped a working product idea in three weeks, got data and customer insights, then stopped the experiment.

I still tell those stories ten years later; they are real and powerful and are what agile is all about.

Why is it important? Well, agile coaching at scale usually starts to remove you from the "coalface" and often means losing direct contact with customers, or you're spread a bit thin and cannot spend the quality time with individual teams. Or sometimes you work through other people and not directly with teams, being one step removed from the action. When this happens, your experience is not direct, meaning you do not learn the lessons as deeply as you would if you were working at the team level.

Years later, when you're coaching larger systems of work, people will know you have that direct experience; they'll also know if you do not. You won't have the stories because you have not been there. So, I repeat, never, ever skip this role.

Your clients in this size system of work will include:

- Product owners
- Scrum masters or team facilitators
- Team members
- Product, delivery, and project managers
- Roles around the team—like designers, finance people, or architects if you're working in software. These roles will be varied, providing many different types of clients for you to coach. Usually these people are in the system of work and their behavior has an impact on the team being able to deliver value.

Your agile learning topics for this role would include the following, which I've put in a recommended, prioritized order, which, of course, you can change to suit your situation. Each topic needs to be understood (you know it) but also practiced (you've done it), and you should have been assessed as competent (you've been checked) by a more experienced mentor:

1. Single-team agile practices and frameworks, e.g., scrum and Kanban
2. Backlog refinement, stories, estimation, definitions of done and prioritization
3. Conducting coaching conversations with people in and around teams; this book
4. Facilitation and working with groups

5. Lean startup
6. Human-centered design
7. DevOps, XP, Lean software development, etc., if you want to work with software teams

There are many, many books, blogs, and websites that will support you with learning these topics. Some accreditation/certification companies also offer courses, but you can do it yourself with the right mentor, then select the accreditations that help you signal to the market you take agile seriously enough to pay for training. So, don't skip the knowledge in the topics above; this is the agile part of agile coaching.

Agile Coaching Medium

Coaching a system of work this size has some additional topics you need to know about and be able to Tell, Show, or advise others on. Working at scale requires the agile coach to see patterns in the additional complexities of the larger system. If you have spent time coaching the small-sized system before moving into this type of role, you will, with the right mentor, be able to apply what you've learned up into the medium system. Often you will have to work with and through other agile coaches and /or scrum masters when taking on this type of role.

This type of role is an important milestone for an agile coach's career journey. It marks the transition towards mastery and should involve helping others who are just starting their journey into agile coaching.

Your clients in this size system of work will include:

- Senior product owners, sponsors, or other leaders/managers
- Senior scrum masters or team facilitators
- Team members
- Product, delivery, program, or project managers

Your learning topics for this role would include the following, which I've put in a recommended, prioritized order, which, of course, you can change to suit your situation:

1. All of the topics from the Agile Coaching Small

2. Agile at scale frameworks, e.g., www.scaledagileframework.com or Large-Scale Scrum www.less.works

3. Lean product management

4. Value stream mapping

5. Conducting coaching conversations with leaders or more senior stakeholders

6. Organization and team design for agile – basic principles

7. Beyond budgeting; www.bbrt.org

8. Again, I'm not going to spend time providing detailed advice on these topics; there are many people who've written books on these agile subjects. Spend some time on YouTube and you can learn the theory; then, with the right mentor, you can learn the associated practices.

What I did want to highlight is how the move from small to medium agile coaching will involve you working on yourself in order to be able to start helping junior coaches follow the path you've traveled. Coaches working at this level think fast, act in the moment, and deliver value consistently; to do this you need to have expert knowledge and skills and the ability to provoke clients towards change. My challenge to you as you start to work in medium roles is to maintain your ability to choose the Open and Hold move as required so you can take the conversation down when needed. You will also need to watch out for the expert habit, where you react instead of responding to requests for help.

Finally, I want to mention the need for a coach to unlearn as they transition their work into a medium-sized system from a small one. When I mentor aspiring medium size agile coaches, they often struggle to let go of thinking in the smaller system; they are required to lift up their perspective and consider the bigger picture. The coach now has to work with and through others to affect change; this skill and being able to see things from a bigger perspective takes time to learn. I would say 12 to 18 months of active mentoring and on-the-job experience is required to learn and unlearn how to transition from coaching a small system to a medium-sized one.

Agile Coaching Large

Coaching in a large system is another ball game all together; it looks more like consulting than agile coaching. Problem solving, designing the framework for the system of work, coaching, and advising executives/leaders will usually be part of this role.

Coaching here relies on deep knowledge of small and medium agile coach roles with eight to ten years' experience to match.

Agile coaches doing this role work more with the intent of the principles of agile, often having to make design decisions that affect thousands of employees and have significant implications for the organization and its competitiveness/effectiveness.

Often coaches working at this level will support and develop a community of agile coaches/practitioners, helping mentor and build the capability for the organization in support of cultural or organizational change programs.

It is beyond the scope of this book to detail what could be involved in this role, but as a career option, it is there and will require all the topics of the two previous role types, usually with the addition of working with executives to link agile ways of working to organizational strategy. Expert-level responsive agile coaching capability is required when working in this role type.

Which Role Is for You?

Up is not always better in agile coaching. In fact, many coaches find their way into one of the above role types and spend their whole career there. Some coaches desire to work in larger systems while others move between role types (like me). Mastering agile coaching will take a lifetime, so please consider this and don't be in a rush to coach larger systems of work. I worked for eight years before moving into a role coaching large systems of work. I've also seen coaches try to move too quickly up into senior roles only to find they are out of their depth.

For now, I'd like you to consider your current aspirations and career assumptions for a moment before reading on; jot some thoughts down in your journal.

Chapter Summary

- There are primarily three types of agile coaching roles: small, medium, and large.

- Each role has specific agile knowledge and skills required combined with specific agile coaching client types.

- Agile coaches are strongly discouraged from skipping working at the team level (small size), as it is where you learn the foundational principles of what agile was originally intended for.

- Coaches can move between the various role sizes but should not be in a rush to move to larger systems of work too soon.

CHAPTER 21.

THE JOURNEY TO BECOMING A RESPONSIVE AGILE COACH

I thought long and hard when writing this book about how I can best explain and bring to life the learning journey of someone developing their responsive agile coaching capability. To solve this, I've decided to use storytelling (a true story) to help you understand what's involved in becoming a responsive agile coach.

I've had the privilege of watching beginner agile coaches I've mentored over the years grow and mature their coaching careers, and I'm going to tell you a story about one of them. I want you to connect to the journey that a beginner usually goes through to grow into a responsive agile coach.

This story is real and involves a few people I've mentored over a five-year period. I've changed some of the details to ensure anonymity. Read it and try to relate it to your story, or at least parts of your story. There is a main character, Steve, who is a combination of three people, including agile coaches and change managers I've previously mentored. There is also Jill, who is the senior agile coach in the story and is a composite of a number of amazing people I've worked with and been mentored by over the last ten years; some of them were coaches, some consultants, others were master facilitators. Enjoy, and remember, all of what you read really happened; it's a true story.

First Day on a New Job

Steve was nervous as he considered what clothes to wear for the day's work ahead; he was always nervous when he started a new contract with a new company. This time it was different though, as he had been hired as a scrum master. Three weeks ago, he didn't know what that meant—strange job title. But as he'd later learned that was what he'd been doing for the past two years; all it meant was that he helped teams implement agile ways of working. This was all new to Steve, but he was sure of one thing: "I'm no master," he said out loud to no one in particular as he looked at himself in the mirror. *I barely have two years' experience working with a team*, he thought in a moment of self-doubt. He called out to his wife as she got their two children their breakfast "Hey, Sally, do you think the Doc Martens are too casual? This is a corporate role."

"Just be yourself!" his wife yelled back from the kitchen.

Easier said than done, Steve thought. *You're not the one who risks looking stupid when everyone else is in a suit and tie and I'm wearing my Docs and a t-shirt.*

As Steve pondered his choice of socks; he recalled his career journey and how he'd arrived where he was. For the past two years, he had been building his capabilities as a team-level agile practitioner. Steve was ambitious, driven, and determined, some would say stubborn. But if anything, he wanted to be recognized as being great at something. Not having earned a degree, Steve left university empty-handed, dropping out in his second year of an economics course to work as a software developer.

Ever since, he had never felt like he had a profession; he was searching for a community where he could be seen as an expert for what he did and respected and rewarded accordingly. Working with agile inside a team for the past two years had shown Steve a glimpse of what a great workplace could be like. Agile as a way of working was what Steve had been looking for in a career. It allowed him to make a difference—having a job where he could enable a culture that got work done but never at the expense of the people who did the work. Steve's beliefs

and values were brought to
life through agile; he loved it
and wanted to learn all there
was about it.

"Goodbye! Wish me luck!"
Steve yelled as he headed out
the door.

"Good luck, and, Steve, just
be yourself. Listen, learn, and don't show that attitude you sometimes get; you only have one chance to make a first impression."

Sally was referring to Steve's attitude of self-righteousness,
which seemed to come out when he felt wronged and "hard-do-
ne-by." He was very conscious of remaining humble as he par-
ticipated in the agile community. He'd seen first-hand what can
happen when your attitude gets ahead of your ability as an agile
practitioner. And as he journeyed into his first day on his new
job, he recalled one such recent experience.

During his recent job hunting, Steve had come across a new
role title he'd never really considered before, "Agile Coach." This
title intrigued Steve, as he loved rugby and always marveled at
the coaches of the major teams directing their troops into battle
against opponents. He wasn't sure this was what an agile coach
did, but given his passion for agile ways of working, Steve went
along to a networking Meetup event to learn more.

The Meetup involved a panel of expert agile coaches being
interviewed by another supposed "expert," and Steve was in
the audience during the Q and A. The facilitator of the event
opened up the floor to questions from the audience, and one
young woman put up her hand and asked: "I've been agile coaching for a year since leaving university and finishing my agile

practitioner two-day course; what tips and advice would you give me to help my career?"

People in the audience actually laughed, mocking the young woman. One of the experts on the panel replied in what could only be described as a condescending tone: "I think it is a bit presumptuous for you to be calling yourself an agile coach; most agile practitioners don't coach until they have at least a few years under their belt. I'd suggest you work as a team-level practitioner for a while longer before thinking about the coaching aspects of your role."

As he recalled that night, Steve felt a chill go down his spine. He felt very similar to the young woman in that he had limited experience, and although he was intrigued by the prospect of becoming an agile coach, he was fearful of being called out as an imposter by the community he was part of. After attending that event, there was no way he'd call himself an agile coach, not after what he saw.

He pushed the negative thoughts out of his mind and headed off to his first day of work at his new employer, NeoBank. He was still nervous but hopeful that this role would be the one to set him up for the next phase in his career.

So, This Is What "Great" Looks Like

Working at NeoBank was very different to Steve's previous role. Very different. On his first day, he was introduced to Jill, and from the very first moment they met, Steve was in awe of her skills. Jill was a senior agile coach, but Steve considered her a magician. She did things that seemed to involve superpowers. Jill achieved outcomes that Steve thought were impossible, and she seemed to be able to solve amazingly complex problems on the spot in front of very senior managers. Steve experienced this in the first hour on his very first day at NeoBank.

Jill marched onto the floor, almost running: "Good morning, everyone. Let's get started! Hey, Bob, it's synch time! Fred, don't make me shame you into coming today." Jill proceeded to stomp around the floor, rounding up everyone, announcing it was time for the daily synch-up meeting.

What then ensued was one of the most amazing feats of facilitation Steve had ever witnessed. Twenty-five people came together at a giant wall full of cards, tape, string, stickers, and pictures of cartoon characters; there was even a bell hanging up. Another 15 people were on video conference from across the globe, all there to align on what was going on in NeoBank's digitization program. 1450 people in 130 teams spread across the world; this is where everyone aligned to connect daily, and Jill was the conductor of this complex orchestra of activity.

Steve watched Jill that first day as she easily handled pushy, almost aggressive behavior, clarifying vague updates provided by underprepared attendees, laughing, being quiet when required, all the way to an emotional celebration marked by the ringing of the bell to celebrate the delivery of a major piece of work for the program. Jill not only had a strong process to guide everyone forward, but the way she managed to room was genius. Steve was inspired and at the same time overwhelmed by Jill's abilities. *How on Earth could I possibly ever perform at that level? How could I ever be able to call myself an agile coach if that is what they need to be able to do?* But as he would soon learn, there was even more to the role of an agile coach; things that Jill did that went far beyond the visible display he saw that first day.

One thing he knew for sure after that first day was that the "expert" at the Meetup was right; to be an agile coach requires a lot more experience and capability than people think. Steve forgot about becoming an agile coach for the moment; it seemed a bit far out of his reach. Anyway, he had a job as a scrum master, and he was going to enjoy it. Safe with his 12-month contract, he could watch, listen, and learn from others who were more experienced.

Call to Adventure

"Really!?" Steve exclaimed. This was at the regular coffee catch-up he had with the small team of scrum masters at Neo-Bank; they were discussing the latest reorganization. Steve's supposed 12-month contract looked like it was not going to last the full 12 months, and his current manager was under pressure to move his entire team into the "new ways of delivering" center of expertise where Jill would run a team of agile coaches.

"I've heard that our manager is on the way out and Jill will be leading all the agile practitioners; she'll be head of capability for agile and we will have to train up and become agile coaches," said Mitch, a fellow scrum master, to the group having coffee. This was Steve's worst nightmare; he didn't want to become a coach. He was happy watching from the sideline, listening and learning from Jill and her coaching team. He was about to complain about how this was so unfair and that he had a contract and should just be allowed to do the job he had been hired for, when Jill walked over and sat down.

"Hey, everyone, what's up?" Steve was always a bit nervous around Jill; she seemed to see through him, able to know his state and ask just the right question to wobble his confidence while at the same time motivating him to be a better version of himself. She then asked everyone a question.

"What's under what you do at work? What's your personal 'WHY' that motivates you to work in agile?"

Steve's immediate response was to make a joke. "Ha! I work to live, not live to work," he said, somewhat awkwardly.

Jill's response was instant and cut straight through his false confidence. "Rubbish, come on, we can be honest here. I know you all aren't just here for the paycheck every week. Steve, I notice how keen you are to listen and learn. I've watched you at morning synch meetings, how you're attentive and open to learning. I know you've done a few certification courses since starting here. Surely, it's not just about working to live; what does the next version of Steve look like, and how can I help make that happen? I'm looking out for people to come and join me in a center of expertise for agile; you're welcome to apply."

Steve instantly knew what he'd done. He'd tried to avoid a conversation about his "inner" world; Jill was checking to see if he could go there and talk on a slightly deeper level about what he did for a living. She wanted to know his "why." Steve blushed slightly at being called out and reflected on the conversation. *Jill has done it again; simultaneously provocative while challenging me to be better. She saw, or maybe had intuition on, what my internal emotions were, and in the moment, cheered me on to grow and develop myself. She was coaching and mentoring me, and it annoyed me for reasons I can't explain, but at the same time, I feel that she cares about me.* Steve stayed quiet. He didn't know why but working with Jill was not something he was ready for.

Steve left the coffee shop. Jill's offer seemed risky compared to staying with what he knew. He decided that he would consult the only person who knew his inner world—his wife, Sally—and get her view of Jill's offer.

Refusal of the Call

Sally sighed heavily as she always did when her husband was like he was now: angry, frustrated, opinionated, and not listening.

"Gosh you're stubborn, Steve!" she said after an hour of discussing Jill's offer over two glasses of wine. "This Jill person sounds amazing! Why don't you want to go learn from her and become an agile coach?"

"You don't understand, Sally; the agile coach title is not something you just self-appoint; it's considered an expert-level role in our industry; I've only been a scrum master for three years, and most of that time I've been faking it. You should see what this Jill person can do; there's no way I can do what she does!

Anyway, I have another four months left on my NeoBank contract; they won't terminate it early because this digitization program is due to run for another year at least."

Steve continued his monologue, not giving his wife the opportunity to get a word in. "Besides, the pay is the same, so what's the point?"

To which Sally responded, "Well, Steve, that's a question only you can answer; what is the point of this whole agile thing you're pursuing in your career? I thought you wanted to be an IT consultant. What's changed?"

This made Steve pause. "You're starting to sound like Jill; she asked me almost the exact same question the other day: what's my WHY?'"

"Well, there you have it, Steve. Maybe you need to get your own story straight about what you go to work for in the first place, then all this career confusion might just solve itself."

"Maybe you're right," Steve responded. "Anyway, for now I just don't feel confident enough to go work with Jill as an agile coach."

And just like that, Steve decided to stay a scrum master.

Five weeks later, sure enough, the reorganization came, and Steve stayed with his current manager. Jill formed her center of expertise, and Steve wasn't part of it. He was content being a scrum master.

At the regular scrum master coffee catch-up, Steve explained his decision to his peers. "I don't want the word 'coach' in my title; scrum masters can do coaching-type work without all the expectation from the agile community. No, I'm safe here in my current role; coaching is not for me."

Meeting with the Mentor

One year later. Steve was growing in confidence; he was pretty sure he had certifications in just about every agile framework out there. If there was a certification available, Steve would have done it. It seemed the only thing that really gave Steve a boost in confidence was another letter after his name. Between going to all the Meetup events to build a strong network, managing to keep his contract going at NeoBank, and getting all his new certifications, Steve was a busy member of the agile community. Something was about to happen that would put Steve onto an entirely different career path, and, of course, it had something to do with Jill.

Steve was getting a bit fed up with his manager, Bob. Although Bob considered Steve to be his top performing scrum master and would often ask him to speak at leadership sessions, it was becoming obvious that this was more about promoting Bob's career than it was about supporting Steve's career goals. As his contract was coming up for renewal, Steve was pondering his next role and what it might be when his cell phone rang. It was Bob; sigh... "Hey, Steve, you'll never guess who just called me demanding that you come work on this important new initiative." Steve knew what he was going to say and secretly was excited, but still he waited to hear it.

"Jill, the super coach from the Agile Center of Excellence; she is OK with me continuing to be your manager while you go and work for her. Looks like everyone is a winner; I've been looking for a way to work with her, and now you can represent my team. This is great; are you excited?"

"Well, I suppose you're not really asking me, are you? So, is this a done deal? What will my job title be?" Steve asked nervously.

"I have no idea; it's up to you, I suppose. Why do you ask? Your pay will get a little bump, so that's good," he continued on before Steve could respond. "Anyway, Jill wants to have a chat with you today, so expect her call. Gotta go. Talk soon, Steve!"

Jill sat across from Steve as they met one-on-one for the first time; this was a more formal setting compared to previous casual coffee encounters.

She opened the meeting. "So, Steve, it's great to finally be working with you. I'll be setting directions for your day-to-day work from now on and boy, have I got a job for you!" Jill then hesitated, leaned back, and paused in a moment of silence.

Steve was a bit puzzled, saying to himself, *What's she doing? I've never seen Jill not know what to say or do; why the silence?* To avoid the awkward moment Steve said, "Yes, I'm super keen to get to work! Bob gave me a few details, but what is it you need me to do?"

Jill's response surprised and challenged Steve. "I tell you what, Steve; let's flip your question. What do you want to do? I want to support you in where you're going, not impose my agenda onto your career. I'm sensing there's something you're not telling me... You seem apprehensive."

Steve considered the question. *There it was again: Jill and her ability to ask just the right question at just the right moment, to both disrupt my thinking but push me to challenge myself.*

Sitting in silence, Steve considered Jill's challenge. He'd heard of servant leadership, empowerment, and those other consultant statements before, and it was in that moment that it all became real for Steve. He had a choice. He was being served/helped to become what he wanted to be; it felt good but forced him to own what he would say next in response to Jill's question.

Steve, all of a sudden, knew what Jill was up to. Sitting in silence, the conversation continued inside his head: *She wants me to say it so that I will own it. Jill wants me to ask for what I want rather than her giving it to me.*

He was suddenly aware of the fact he was facing a previously unseen fear. *She's inviting me to become an agile coach.* In that moment, he hesitated; he didn't know why he was so scared. Something in his gut was telling him that he should say yes.

Jill noticed his hesitation. "Steve, I'll mentor you, and it'll be fun, you'll see; but you have to want it, Steve. Do you?" Jill was then silent. She sat opposite Steve, holding eye contact, fully present and attentive, awaiting Steve's response, no judgement or expectation.

Steve smiled inwardly. "Yep, let's do it, Jill. I want to become an agile coach."

Stepping into the Unknown

What became clear to Steve very quickly was the type of game he had to play as an agile coach. It was a bigger league with more at stake. In a word, Steve was expected to be a leader, to bring tools, techniques, and practices to help resolve complex problems, then lead others through a process of change. Luckily, Steve was well equipped with all he'd learned from the many courses he'd been through and the years of experience he'd gained and was keen to apply his newfound knowledge in the real world. Jill was preparing to give him all the opportunities he needed. Little did Steve know that he was about to work on an initiative that would be the most stressful but rewarding role of his career to date.

Steve got to see Jill in action, and the more he worked with her, the more he realized how much he had to learn; more specifically, he was becoming aware of how she worked with others, not just what she did. "I watch her work and I still can't work out how she does it," Steve said to a fellow coach over a coffee. "She comes into the room and somehow generates... I don't know what you'd call it...a vibe, energy, maybe curiosity. People are just interested in trying something new. I try to do the same, using the same facilitation agenda, and the next day I get 'feedback' from people saying I didn't 'read the room.' I'm sick of the same feedback over and over."

As for Jill, she was reflecting on her work with Steve so far during a conversation with one of her peers. "Steve never asks for feedback, and I find myself having to deliver Steve tips and advice in a less formal manner, usually over a beer at the end of the week."

Her colleague responded with: "Do you think he'll make a great agile coach?"

To which Jill responded, "It all depends on him; he will have to face his own behaviors at some point if he wants to progress. He's great 90 percent of the time, but when under pressure, you can see

him losing patience, and everyone in the room knows it too. The problem is that he's unaware that everyone has noticed his self-control issues when facilitating. So, I'm looking for ways to raise both his self-awareness and his awareness of how he's impacting his clients. He has all the technical skills, certificates, and accreditations; hell, he's got more of them than I have!"

Six months later. Steve continued to get advice from Jill but thought he was ready to take the next step and work more independently; plus, he'd received an offer to work in another part of the company, out from under Jill, with his own initiative. He wanted to start working with leaders and was keen to roll out his newfound knowledge from a scaled agile course he'd just completed. The opportunity to lead a program of work as the senior coach came up, and Steve jumped on it. He met with Jill to discuss.

"Hi, Jill. What do you think of this new role I'm considering?"

Jill was patient and sensed Steve needed to explore options on his own; he'd stopped considering her advice like he used to. It was not that he had become arrogant; it was that Steve did not see the work Jill had done to date behind the scenes to set Steve up for success in his role with her. He simply didn't know what he didn't know and despite everything Jill had said to him, he had stopped listening and was impatient to be a senior agile coach. Jill considered her response before replying to Steve.

"Steve, let me respond by asking you to consider two questions: What do you think are the key capabilities a great agile coach needs to succeed? And what do you think you need to work on to have those key capabilities?"

Steve quickly shot back, slightly defensively: "I don't think that's the issue here; I haven't had the right level of support from the leaders where I am currently to do the things I know I can do."

Jill, somewhat unimpressed with this answer, was blunt in her response: "Steve, what if, just for the moment, we assumed everything that's an issue for you right now in your current role was 100 percent your fault?"

Now Steve was really quite upset. "Well, we know that's not the case; what's the point of your question?"

Jill was not getting through; Steve seemed determined to not consider his part in the problems he was facing. She considered this an opportunity for Steve to learn an important (hard) lesson about what she had seen in him for the last year they'd been working together, but it seemed today was not the day Steve would learn this lesson. The meeting ended.

The next year was a difficult one for Steve.

"You don't understand!" Steve exclaimed to his wife as they were having dinner one evening after a particularly tough day for Steve. "It feels like everyone around me at the moment is bullying me, bossing me around, and telling me what to do. I'm the victim here."

Sally had patiently listened to Steve complain for a few weeks now and was growing increasingly concerned for his health. His stress levels were not sustainable, and he was drinking too much.

"Maybe you need a change, Steve. It's not really working since you moved away from Jill. What does she think about what's happening?"

"She just says it's all my fault and I should accept responsibility for the situation I'm in. I thought that if I went to this role, I'd have a chance to do something on my own and learn to stand on my own two feet, out from underneath Jill's shadow."

"Well, she does cast a big shadow," Sally responded, "but something needs to change. Steve, please think about what you can do."

Later that week, things went horribly wrong for Steve.

Typing the email, Steve knew it would cause trouble, but his fingers kept typing. Something in him was cheering him on to vent off his frustration. He'd tell this person just how they weren't adhering to the values of agile. He spent another few minutes crafting the email and hesitated for a minute, considering... "No, he deserves to be told; it's my job to tell him," he said to no-one in particular as he hit "SEND."

Three months later, when considering contract renewals, Steve's manager, Bob, read the feedback he'd been receiving on Steve. Included were notes from a long conversation with one of Steve's coaching customers within NeoBank: "Dogmatic, inflexible, opinionated, and unable to apply the social skills required to work with senior stakeholders." Bob had no choice with such pressures on his budget; Steve's role as an agile coach had come to an end at NeoBank.

Approaching the Turning Point

Sally and Steve were discussing the recent events at NeoBank and working through Steve's employment options.

"I'm going to go back to my old role; they're happy to have me back to work as a team scrum master. I just need to get my health back and reflect on the whole NeoBank thing."

Sally felt for Steve. He'd thrown his energy and effort into becoming an agile coach. "It's OK, darling. You learned a lot from Jill, didn't you?"

Steve reflected. "Not as much as I could have; I've come to the conclusion that I'm not a good listener."

This sparked an idea from Sally. "Steve, I remember hearing about this 'coaching for life and work' course my HR friend recently went on. She said it was awesome; she learned a lot about listening. Maybe you should check it out?"

Steve didn't respond.

"Steve! Are you even listening to me?"

"Sorry, I was fiddling with my phone. What did you say?" Steve said, much to his wife's frustration.

Facing Your Fears

"OK, Steve, now it's your turn to share back to the group; what did you learn from the exercise?" Steve reflected on the course so far. He'd signed up for a "Working with Conflict in Agile" seminar and he was getting way more than he had bargained for. Something had opened up for him when they had to role play a typical conflict in the workplace. In the role play, he was being bossed about by a demanding manager.

"Well, I got triggered, I reacted, got angry, and stopped listening. I was too emotional to process the situation and use the techniques you taught us," Steve responded, almost in tears. He was surprised with how emotional he'd become and how quickly he'd been overwhelmed from the pretend role-play scenario. *What the hell is wrong with me? This is just a stupid seminar!* he thought to himself, almost ashamed at showing such vulnerability to total strangers he'd met only the day prior.

All of Steve's training and development work had been focused on learning new knowledge, techniques, and agile practices.

Sure, he'd learned presentation skills and facilitation tactics, but this? This was completely different; he'd lost control and was at a loss as to why.

He found some courage and asked the course facilitator, "What's going on? What do you think is happening to me, and why do you think I've had such a strong reaction to the simple role play?"

"You are very lucky and fortunate, Steve. What happened is almost the best outcome for a course like this. To be able to observe yourself being triggered in this safe learning environment allows you to better understand who you are and how you're affected in certain situations. I understand you're a coach; well, coaching is all about managing yourself so you can be present to serve the person or people you're coaching. To answer your question, I would guess that the role play is pointing to something that, if you can understand it, will help improve your coaching dramatically. I would say that whatever got you emotional is an important aspect of your values that someone has not respected, hence your reaction and inability to be rational. What do you feel is the root cause of the response you experienced during the role play?"

This shook Steve; he was being asked to say out loud what had been so emotional that it caused him to "lose it." He drew a deep breath and considered his answer...

"I didn't like being told what to do; I felt disrespected."

The course facilitator gave Steve his full attention but was silent, leaving space for Steve should he wish to continue.

Silence for another 10 seconds felt like an hour for Steve. The facilitator waited.

"Well, I've done all the courses and I know agile theory and practice. Who is this person to tell me what to do? I might not have a degree, but I know my stuff."

Silence for another 10 seconds felt like another hour for Steve.

"Go on," said the facilitator.

"I guess I feel I have the right to be seen as the expert, but I still feel I'm proving myself as a coach; I still feel like I'm a fake. When I was being told what to do, it made me feel worthless and brought to my attention that I don't have any degrees or other university qualifications. I thought that agile was my thing, so why is this person bossing me around like they know it all?"

"Awesome, Steve. So what's the lesson here in terms of you knowing a bit more about yourself?"

"I need to not take everything so personally; not everyone is challenging me, and I need to stop projecting my low self-confidence onto the people I'm coaching—that's for starters! I'm pretty sure I'm a terrible listener because I think I know it all and don't think I've got anything to learn from those around me. The list goes on; this has been a real breakthrough for me. A real eye opener on issues I didn't even know were there. I'm starting to see I have a lot more work to do if I want to become a great agile coach and I also see why some of my previous mentors were able to do the things I, until now, thought were magic. But now I know that they've just done a lot of work on themselves and know how to manage their own triggers. It all makes so much more sense now."

"Wow, Steve, you really did have a deep insight from the role play. My experience is that this was probably building up for a long time, and today it just burst through. But you had to want to do the work, and today you did; you put yourself out there. You allowed yourself to be a little vulnerable and played a good game today, so well done. Everyone, give Steve a round of applause."

Steve had previously considered this type of course as fluffy, or as he liked to joke with some of his peers at work, 'woo-woo' soft stuff. Having been brought up in a culture where talking about how you feel was not really the done thing in the workplace, Steve was not skilled at working with or utilizing emotions as part of his coaching role. But he was starting to realize that emotions had a lot to do with coaching.

He was sensing that he had suddenly been given the secret ingredient to becoming a great agile coach; something that's not listed in any of the agile frameworks or certifications. Right then and there, Steve started writing down his thoughts on the newfound and previously unseen capabilities he now knew (really knew) were critical for his professional development. Although he tried, Steve struggled to get the words out on paper.

Steve could now see the importance of what he'd learned from the conflict workshop and role plays, but what specifically it was that he'd learned still needed to be clarified in his own words.

The Reward

Sally was waiting patiently for Steve to announce what his big insight was that he absolutely had to tell her about, but he seemed to be struggling to articulate it in words.

"Something to do with emotions, listening, respecting other people's opinions, being authentic about where I'm up to in my development. Oh, and I really need to lose the attitude I seem to be carrying about not having a degree." Steve was talking quickly and was very excited about his new view of himself.

"Right then, so what are you going to do, Steve? Of course, I could have told you all this without you having to go to a workshop to learn it, but hey, I'm just your wife; what would I know?" she sarcastically remarked in jest.

"Haha," Steve responded. "Well, I'm going to look into emotions and how to work with them. That, I think, is the most important thing. Also, I need to be more... What's the word? Conscious? No... You know what I'm saying, Sally... Make what I haven't been seeing more visible to myself?"

"Aware?" said Sally. "Aware of how you get in your own way of being a good listener and when you get that look on your face that tells everyone else that you're getting an attitude?" She raised an eyebrow.

"It's like you're telling me I should be more aware of me, myself?" Steve responded.

"Yes, let's just call it self-awareness." Sally finished the conversation as they headed into the bathroom to get ready for bed.

Steve proceeded to his laptop and started browsing the internet. After 30 minutes of searching and reading, he Googled "how to be more self-aware," and the following results came back:

1. Look at yourself objectively.
2. Keep a journal.
3. Write down your goals, plans, and priorities.
4. Perform daily self-reflection.
5. Practice meditation and other mindfulness habits.
6. Take personality and psychometric tests.
7. Ask trusted friends to describe you.

OK, I can't do all of these, so I'll start with number four and number seven, Steve committed to himself. Satisfied he'd found the missing ingredient required for becoming a great agile coach, he shut down his laptop, but in the back of his mind he could not help but wonder if this was just the tip of a much bigger iceberg, a larger "blind spot" he had not previously seen. He pushed it out of his mind for now and joined his wife in bed.

The Road Back

Upon returning to work, Steve started to see all the situations where he wasn't being self-aware. He felt like he had been shown the secret to being awesome and threw himself into a development plan focusing on self-awareness.

Many courses, workshops, and seminars later, Steve was making progress and had been receiving positive feedback on his coaching work. He'd even hired himself a professional mentor/coach to support him, resulting in Steve being significantly more centered and calm when under pressure. His wife even said he'd lost his attitude.

Twelve months later, Steve was presenting at a conference on how self-awareness had greatly improved his ability to listen and respond to others when working with senior leadership teams.

He was presenting on how his self-awareness had turned into a superpower of sorts. He was highlighting how his newfound ability to witness himself getting upset and sense the impact of his actions on others has enabled him to be more effective with leaders. Mid-way through the conference presentation, Steve noticed his previous mentor, Jill, in the audience. For some reason, this made him anxious. He remembered back to his work at NeoBank and how he had not performed well in the exact capability he was presenting his conference talk on.

Jill watched on, thinking, *This is really interesting. I'm hopeful Steve has learned to listen and keep calm under these conditions; I wonder if anything in him has shifted since I last saw him.*

Steve froze, nervous, and fumbled his presentation; he couldn't focus with Jill looking on. It was then that he used what he'd been learning about self-awareness. He checked his posture, took a deep breath from his belly, paused a moment, centered, and relaxed; he refocused.

Steve recovered and finished, albeit a bit wobbly compared to when he had practiced his presentation earlier in the week.

Jill came over after the presentation had finished. "Hi, Steve. You've really invested in yourself. I can see the shift, and it's incredible!"

"Really? I thought I blew it," Steve replied.

"Not at all. You're facing your fear, putting yourself out there, being vulnerable, and obviously growing as a person and as an agile coach."

Slightly humbled, Steve blushed.

Before he could say anything, Jill was talking again. "Would you be interested in coming and interviewing for a role my director has opening up? I think you might be ready, Steve."

"Ready for what? Sounds like a challenge," said Steve.

"Well, your previous agile coach role was really just implementing the processes of agile across a number of teams. This role requires leadership coaching. All that means is you have to be able to work with and influence executives on how they approach their jobs and have them support the agile transformation."

"And you think I'm ready for that?" Steve was not entirely confident and certainly not as sure as Jill was in terms of him being ready.

The Final Test

Steve had never been both so nervous and so calm at the same time. His self-awareness work had stopped being an extra thing he did and had become just part of how he invested in becoming a better person as well as a great agile coach. It was part of who he was and not something he did to get better roles as a coach.

Leading up to the day of the job interview, he had read and reread the job responsibilities Jill had given him, and he knew that this was the role he'd been aiming to get his entire career—senior agile coach, working with executives to enable an enterprise transformation.

Jill had warned him that the interview would be role-played and involved a pressurized situation where he had to coach an executive who was leading a team of agile teams. Jill's manager would be there, and he was tough on applicants, so Steve would need to bring his "A game" if he was going to be successful.

Steve walked confidently into the interview room with upright posture, managing his breathing.

Jill's manager looked at Steve and opened the interview. "Steve let's jump straight into role play. I'm your executive, and you're coaching me on why I need a coach. And, Steve, I'm just warning you, we have some interesting execs here at NeoBank, so I'm going to play a bit rough just to put you through your paces. Fair?"

"Sure, no problem. Let's go," responded Steve. Now he was nervous for real.

Jill's manager opened the role play, taking on the persona of a rather terse and change-resistant executive. "Hi, Steve. My name is Fred, and I've only got one question for you. What are you going to teach me that I don't already know? With due respect, I've got an MBA and a degree in accounting; I see here you haven't even been to university. I'm pretty busy, so what's on your mind?"

This completely threw Steve. He was immediately triggered. With that one sentence, he was back to being who he was that first day at NeoBank; his confidence disappeared, and he felt anger starting to boil up from his stomach, threatening to derail the interview.

Steve glanced over at Jill, and their eyes met. She must have been projecting something along the lines of: "You can do this; I know you can."

In such a state, Steve only had one chance to pick one technique to bring him back from where he was heading—a disaster. He took a moment and picked the technique he knew would save him. Steve chose to stop, just for that moment, and do nothing, although it felt like an eternity. Doing nothing opened up a tiny space between the challenging question the interviewing manager asked and the angry reaction that almost happened.

It was in that space that Steve executed some of the self-awareness practices that he had learned. He centered his body weight, then he put both his hands flat onto the desk and said to himself, *How can I best serve this person in this moment?* It was a compassion technique he'd been working on. Then the answer came. Steve considered the person; they were projecting status, being forceful. He instantly realized that being more confident was not the answer. *Lower my status and just start helping.*

"Hi Fred; happy to keep this simple and short as I know you're busy. I'm here to help get things done for you. What's your top priority right now?"

And just like that, Steve came back from the brink of reacting. He was tested to his limit; he had to call upon all he had been practicing over the last few years of development. The interview proceeded along with Steve keeping a calm, professional tone and using all of his learned knowledge and skills as an agile coach—the practices and patterns of agile but with the added power of self-awareness.

As Jill watched Steve throughout the interview, she could not help but smile to herself. It was almost like looking at a different person. Steve had a quiet confidence that was part of who he was, not some trick he'd learned to convince someone at an interview; Steve was being authentic.

Return as the "Expert"

A year had passed since the job interview; Steve had got the role and was thriving. He looked back in his mind over the last three years—the role Jill had played in his success, how he had faced his innermost demons and insecurities, and the investment in time and effort to learn and practice new skills.

Steve was starting to be less opinionated and more curious; he was starting to give less advice and ask more questions with leaders. In short, Steve was deepening how he coached. Steve coached people on why they work and helped them (especially leaders) align their personal values with NeoBank's objectives. Of course, he still did a lot of coaching where he was called upon for agile expertise, tips, and advice, but now he had a more flexible suit of capabilities he could draw upon to enable the adoption of agile.

Later that week, Steve was at a Meetup event for agile coaches and was on the panel as a so-called "expert" when a question was put to him from the audience.

"I've been working with a team now for two years as a scrum master. What does it take to become an agile coach?"

Steve smiled at the irony but had such empathy for the person asking the question; he was surprised at how he was instantly energized at wanting to help this person find their path to becoming a great agile coach. He responded, "Well, let me tell you about my story..."

CHAPTER 22.

WHAT WE LEARNED FROM STEVE'S JOURNEY

> *"A ship is always safe at shore, but that is not what it is built for."*
>
> — Albert Einstein.

You Will Step Across Into the Unknown

Becoming an agile coach requires the development of hard skills, like knowledge of agile practices, as well as other tacit, softer skills that are more closely associated with your personal traits, attitude, and style of behavior (habits). It is these softer elements that require you to face feedback from others (as Steve did) without reacting or getting defensive. The irony is you have to take it personally for such feedback to be effective and disrupt your status-quo (provoke you).

Often the iceberg metaphor is used to contrast what we see and what is visible to others versus what is not in view and is unconscious and unknown to us. Einstein implies we are built to be adventurers; as part of your agile coach development, be prepared to go into uncharted territory to places that are below the "waterline" of the iceberg. So, right now, your values and identity are not visible to you. This book is highlighting to you that in order to become a responsive agile coach, you are invited to work with and (probably) alter some of the items that are below your current waterline; things that relate to your attitudes and sense of identity. Being an agile expert is only one half of being a responsive agile coach; the other part is the work you do to change yourself through periodically getting out of your comfort zone. One of this book's contributors, Fiona Tibballs, takes this so seriously that she publishes a blog post every week on how to get out of your comfort zone. She interviews people who are doing activities that put them into uncharted territory; by sharing these stories she encourages others to do the same and learn.

You Will Face Multiple Nemeses

There are many voices, both real and in our own heads, that hold us back from fulfilling our potential. Three common voices that hold us back in our journeys are the voice of judgement, the voice of cynicism, and the voice of fear.

Sharing an opinion that could be wrong risks raising the voice of judgement. Opening up for a conversation on your emotional state can result in the voice of cynicism. Going to the edge of how you define yourself and your purpose can evoke the voice of fear. Steve faced all of these during his journey, but he prevailed, grew as a person and as a professional, and in the process learned who he was and who he was becoming.

Often Steve faced his nemeses due to circumstances or opportunities that he encountered; that's normal, and that's life. So, expect to face these voices should you decide to journey into the unknown and pursue a career in agile coaching.

As coaches it's our job to help transform other people's mindsets and take them on a journey of change; to do that we need to know the territory so we can guide others through the same territory.

Continuous Learning and Practice

Agile coaches have lots to learn—lots! Beginner coaches can get overwhelmed, but there is a sequence of things to discover, and there are many learning pathways to acquire that knowledge. The key point I want to make here is Steve's continuous application of what he was learning. There's a cycle of "know it, do it" that I encourage all coaches to follow. Always look to apply knowledge into an action of doing (practice it) with others and get feedback on your performance, preferably directly after applying the knowledge.

What was in the way of Steve becoming a responsive agile coach? Sure, he had to learn some things and practice his agile ceremonies, but the real barrier was not knowledge or skill but his habits and reactions.

Although acquiring new knowledge is always a good idea, there's a turning point in your career when you realize all of a sudden that learning more things that are "out there" is not going to help you progress. The work that is required is internal. Steve encountered this when he started getting feedback on his facilitation; he needed to change his attitude in order to improve his performance.

Working with Others (Including a Mentor)

Steve worked out that he couldn't journey on his own; companions and a guide were required to navigate unknown territory, face his nemeses, and prevail. Adventures are also better when the experience is shared with others. Steve's wife, Jill, and his community of scrum masters together with the Meetups he attended were all critical to him learning his biggest lessons.

Soft Skills and Self-management

Steve changed his ineffective approach when engaging with leaders; he developed increased levels of situational awareness and through purposeful, repeated practice heightened his ability to "read the room" and respond in the moment to signals from those around him.

Steve's biggest development outcome was his ability to regulate his own state; stay calm when his cues were triggered by people who "rubbed him the wrong way." He navigated his way through this without derailing his career. He did this by utilizing high levels of awareness of his internal state in the moment, non-judgmentally accepting things as they happened, and then responding to de-escalate his state away from overly emotional reactions.

Chapter Summary

- Developing your capability to deliver responsive agile coaching is a journey usually measured in years not months.

- You may need to change who you consider yourself to be in order to develop responsiveness.

- During a career of development, you will face challenges, and this is expected. It is through adversity and a willingness to venture into the unknown that you will grow and learn to become more responsive to the cues that would have previously triggered an unhelpful reaction in you.

References and Further Reading

1. www.scrum.org/resources/scrum-guide

2. https://less.works/

3. https://www.scaledagileframework.com/#

4. Craig Larman and Bas Vodde, *Scaling Lean & Agile Development: Thinking and Organizational Tools for Large-Scale Scrum*, (Pearson Education, 2008).

5. Donald G. Reinertsen, *The Principles of Product Development Flow: Second Generation Lean Product Development*, (Celeritas Publishing, 2009).

6. Dean Leffingwell, *Agile Software Requirements: Lean Requirements Practices for Teams, Programs, and the Enterprise*, (Pearson Education, 2010).

7. Go to www.responsiveagile.coach to learn with others who have read or are reading this book; you can also visit www.responsiveagilecoaching.com for up-to-date content, downloads, and templates.

PART VI
RESPONSIVE AGILE COACHING CAPABILITY

Introduction

Together we have defined responsive agile coaching, shown you what it looks like, and given you practices, helping make the theory and concepts real. Now, finally, it's time to summarize what you can do to build your capability. To start this chapter I'll present the entire Responsive Agile Coaching model, showing the eight steps that are contained within the four moves together with the single end point of the model, all in one big beautiful illustration from Simon Kneebone, who created all of the artwork in this book. In this illustration you can also see the open MIND, HEART and WILL dimensions to give you the complete picture.

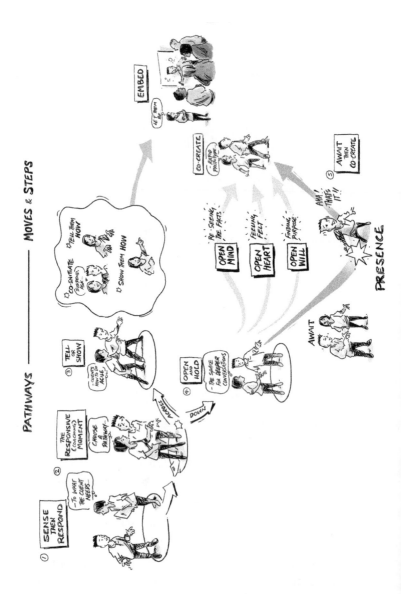

PATHWAYS — MOVES & STEPS

PRESENCE

The task I want to help you undertake now is to plan how you are going to develop areas where you're not yet as proficient as you'd like to be, while also unlearning where required.

CHAPTER 23.

CREATING A LEARNING AND UNLEARNING PLAN

Overview of the Approach

As I sit here writing this chapter, I am on the train, coming home from work, having just run a three-day workshop for scrum masters. My role was to establish a capability uplift and mentoring program for the 70 most senior agile-at-scale practitioners across the company. Today I was with nineteen participants; some of which were coaching and supporting the operations of large systems of work (1000 – 3000 people), half were in medium size systems (100 – 300 people), and there were three people who were new to their role. The approach I'm using to achieve learning outcomes for these agile practitioners is what I'm going to share with you now. It's an approach I've been using and refining for a few years now; I recently had the opportunity to formalise it when asked to internally develop

50 agile team coaches over a twelve-month period. So, it has been well-tested in the field.

The development approach I use consists of three parts:

1. **Community**: working with a mentor and peers to get support and feedback
2. **Learning**: acquiring the knowledge and skills required for your role
3. **Unlearning**: letting go of or modifying old habits

It is common for readers to see a list such as this one and think they can pick and choose what item(s) is best for their situation, then work on that aspect, but to deliver responsive agile coaching, I recommend you work through all three areas of this development plan. Often people are drawn to do more of what they are comfortable with. I have many coaches who love learning—reading, attending courses, watching videos, etc., (point 2) but then fail to do the work on themselves, refusing to unlearn unhelpful habits (point 3).

Likewise, I see lots of coaches who are prolific networkers; they attend every Meetup, talk at conferences, and post to community forums (point 1) but then fail to actually try new things in the workplace (point 2).

Then there are the agile coaches who do a tremendous amount of deep personal development (point 3) but do not learn the agile knowledge and skills (point 2) required to deliver agile coaching.

The saddest example is the loner who thinks they can learn, read, go to Meetups, and even do the deep personal work such as mindfulness but fail to connect with a mentor. This is a hard and long path to becoming a great agile coach; I know this path because I've walked it. For many years, I resisted being active in the community and refused to work with mentors; too proud, arrogant, and stubborn. I completely changed my approach in the last few years, and my learning, agile coaching practice, and career has benefited greatly. Please take my advice; get a mentor as your first action after reading this chapter.

I recommend that you do all of the items in the above list; don't pick and choose the ones you are comfortable with. Let's go through each one now to give you a bit more detail and guidance on how to put your plan together.

Build Your Community

Sometimes this is called "finding your tribe," but it means the same thing: be part of a community that will support your learning. I've started a community for responsive agile coaching (www.responsiveagile.coach) and built a tribe around the ideas in this book; you're welcome to join.

Being part of a community also requires you to learn by helping and supporting others to grow too. In addition to being an active community member, there is one critical element to your learning approach that I want to emphasize: your mentor.

The one thing I'm certain of is you cannot become a responsive agile coach without the help of a mentor. Yes, I'm that certain. Why? Well, you need feedback and lots of it to become good at agile coaching. Mentors bring you down to earth when you think you have it all worked out, helping you to avoid the infamous Dunning-Kruger effect.[1] This effect is very common in agile coaching; here's a short definition:

"A mental reasoning bias in which people assess their ability as greater than it is. This effect comes from the inability of people to recognize their lack of ability. Without the self-awareness, people cannot objectively evaluate their competence or incompetence."

You need a mentor to ensure you do not become deluded and think you are better at agile coaching than you really are. Interactions with a community of practitioners also helps keep you on track with the latest ideas while ensuring you know what you don't know.

Like other knowledge-worker roles, self-awareness for agile coaches is critical for effectiveness, so mentors are a safe way to obtain honest and constructive feedback on your efforts to grow and learn as you build your agile coaching capabilities.

When I hire coaches, I'm on the lookout for the Dunning-Kruger effect in applicants. To test if they have fallen to this effect, I look for their ability to be vulnerable and willingness to admit that they do not know it all. One way I know that they are open to learning is if they have a mentor and can say they do not know the answers to all my questions. Working with a mentor is a very important relationship due to the humility it builds in you as a coach. Working with a mentor also reduces the risk of the Dunning-Kruger effect impacting your coaching.

Great mentors are available to pair with you as you coach, conduct role-plays to test your capability, teach you from their experience, and act as a career guide. They can be hard to find but are essential for your learning. If you cannot arrange a formal mentor, then crowd-source one from various places, Meetups, online, or wherever, but don't assume you can grow on your own.

Organizing Your Learning

There's a lot of agile theory as well as practices and techniques to learn when you're building your agile coaching career. Often, I have coaches coming up to me, asking for advice on the next course they should take to improve their chances of progression into more senior roles. Which brings up an important topic we need to discuss; gaining certificates to get a job versus learning skills to be great at agile coaching.

Often the two are at odds with each other. Getting numerous certificates onto your resume to signal your investment in your profession to recruiters is important, but it is more important to gain the right mix of skills to actually deliver agile coaching.

The way I enable my mentees to learn new skills is a three-phase approach: have them learn the theory, have them apply theory into practice, and then, once they've practiced for a while, have them teach it back to me. It's a simple method but one I've used many, many times with hundreds of agile practitioners.

Let me simplify it for you with ten easy-to-follow steps:

Ten steps to organize your learning:

1. Choose the system of work that you are aiming to deliver agile coaching into (small, medium, or large).

2. Find a person who has experience delivering agile coaching in the size system you're aspiring to work in; ask them to be your mentor. Don't skip this step.

3. Build a learning backlog of items you need to know and do as part of your next role; your mentor will know and advise which are to be prioritized.

4. Create a four-column table (Kanban) with headings across the four columns: backlog; know; do; teach.

5. Work with your mentor to prioritize items into each column of your learning Kanban.

6. Limit the number of items in each column to only one or two and ensure each item is consistent in size and complexity.

7. As you progress, move items along from the "know" column into the "do" column to show that you're practicing the item.

8. Do each item (practice) at least three times with feedback from your mentor and/or a peer.

9. Once you've practiced an item, test yourself by teaching (tell or show) your mentor or someone else who can give you feedback.

10. Periodically review your level of competence and confidence for each item and refine your backlog of learning items.

Learning kanban

Comments/notes for this canvas

Role size I aspire to:
☐ Small (2-30)
☐ Medium (31-300)
☐ Large (301-1300)

Notes: _____

Learning backlog
Prioritized with mentor

What Knowledge
I need to acquire to Tell

What Competence
do I need to Show?

What do I want to
be able to **Teach?**

Often the timing of opportunity for the role you want versus how ready you are to do the role are not in sync (in fact it's usually the norm). So, at some point, you'll need to make a "leap of faith" and work slightly beyond your current proficiency (out of your comfort zone). When this happens (and it will), your mentor will be there to help you navigate into the unknown as you learn your way forward. This is the secret: having a trusted mentor when you are at the limit of what you know and can do provides a "safety net" for your competency and a sounding board during difficult times.

The balance between when to make the leap of faith and when to hold back and keep learning is for you to manage with your mentor; they'll know when you're ready. Coaches applying for roles when they are not ready is a problem in the agile coach profession. It has led to a lot of imposter agile coaches who suffer from the Dunning-Kruger effect. So, please be honest with yourself and work with a mentor because taking a job you're not ready for only leads to low performance and could result in a major career setback if your professional reputation is negatively impacted.

Organizing Your Unlearning

To make room for new learnings and capabilities it is important to recognize what has to be let go of. Unlearning requires a certain amount of self-awareness; specifically, the cues and routines associated with unhelpful habits such as those mentioned in chapters 17 and 18. So, your first task as a coach is to become feedback friendly; solicit and seek feedback on how you are affecting those around you. By doing this you will be able to then assess where your unlearning opportunities lie.

Unlearning can be very specific, simple actions, such as tone of voice or hand gestures that are too assertive as you express your opinion. Or it could be personality traits that are your unlearning opportunity; for example, people who find comfort when they're in control or have the right solution often find it difficult to execute the Open and Hold move in a coaching conversation.

Unlearning in my experience is well suited to an experiment-based approach. Planning and conducting experiments that are time-bound allow you to try new habits and behaviors with the aim of simply "seeing what happens." For example, when you feel the urge to provide a solution, ask the client an open question, such as: "I have lots of thoughts on this, but I'm interested in yours." Then be silent, maintain an open mind, and see what happens. Doing this for two weeks and keeping a journal of insights will start to generate ideas for unlearning opportunities for you.

A recent unlearning for me came when someone made a joke during a workshop I was facilitating. The participant said, "You're a bit scary, Niall," followed by a nervous chuckle.

My intuition alarm bells gave me a signal that this was pointing to something. So, I walked across the classroom, sat down next to this person, slowed down my pace of talking and said, "Really? That's interesting. Tell me more."

She responded by saying, "Well, Niall, you're so full-on, open about your feelings and emotions, confident, and enthusiastic. We're scared to ask questions or challenge anything you have to say. Also, when I share personal insights with you in private, you then replay them out to the entire class of people. I feel embarrassed."

This floored me and revealed a massive blind spot I hadn't seen before. I was destroying the level of psychological safety in my own workshops!

This set off a two- to three-month effort to unlearn my propensity to "overshare" and expect everyone to instantly have an open HEART. I had to learn to share personal insights more carefully and respect what people discussed with me in private. Everyone has unlearning opportunities; you just need to be on the lookout for them.

Learning/Unlearning Canvas

Using a canvas to capture complex ideas on a single page is not a new concept and has been utilized in many and varied ways; business models, product ideas, strategy, managing change, etc., have all used this approach.

I suggest you put together a canvas to represent your current learning/unlearning goals. It is a neat way to capture all your intent and activity on a page as you work with your mentor.

Let me show you an example I've used with agile coaches and practitioners.

Role size I aspire to:
- ☐ Small (2-30)
- ☐ Medium (31-300)
- ☐ Large (301-1300)

Notes: _____

Developing your **Agile** knowledge/skill

What **Knowledge** I need to acquire to Tell

What **Competence** do I need to Show?

What do I want to be able to **Teach?**

Responsiveness

Respond vs react %

How do I **Open** deeper conversations?

How do I **Tell or Show** using the best approach and timing?

How do I **Hold** the space and deeply listen?

How do I **Await** for Presence?

Developing your **Coaching** skills

How do I **Embed** new ways of working?

How do I **Co-create** new ways of working with clients?

Unlearning box

When this happens _____
I will _____
Instead of _____
So that _____

The left-hand side summarizes the goals you have for learning the knowledge and skills of agile; these underpin your capability to Tell and Show clients the answers to their agile adoption problems while also supporting your co-creation work should the conversation follow the downward pathway. I've added a Teach section to this canvas to assess your ability to educate others; this is a great way to embed your own learning.

The right-hand side captures all of the other moves in the Responsive Agile Coaching model and provides space to visualize where your current focus is as you develop your ability to deliver responsive agile coaching to your clients.

To round out the canvas I've included two boxes: one for your unlearning goals and another to track your efforts at responding versus reacting when choosing a conversation pathway.

I suggest you prepare a canvas similar to this one and update it with Post-it notes that outline your experiments in each area. Then, every time you meet with your mentor, discuss insights gained and use these to plan your next set of experiments. This, combined with a journal to capture insights and reflections, should provide you with the tools to move your development forward with the support of your community and access to a mentor. Good luck. I wish you all the best in your journey!

Chapter Summary

- Development involves three parts; community, learning and unlearning. All are recommended to ensure a comprehensive development plan.

- Finding a mentor is the first and most important step in your development.

- Canvases are a lean method to organize, visualize and manage your learning / unlearning activities and experiments.

CHAPTER 24.

RESPONSIVE AGILE COACHING IN AN ORGANIZATION

I want to take a moment now to discuss what the Responsive Agile Coaching model would look like if it were to be scaled across into the broader organization. If your job is to be a leader of people, an organizational change manager, or a transformation consultant, you will probably be interested in how this model can be applied at scale to enable cultural change.

So, this is a brief chapter to help address some of these topics and provide some advice on what it would mean if everybody across an organization was having responsive agile coaching conversations.

(Agile) Coaching as a Culture

What I found interesting when reading the research literature on organizational change was my growing realization that agile coaching and associated practices of agile at scale were supposed to be the missing piece in the puzzle that would provide the link between the systems theory (of creating learning organizations) and the reality of what happens day to day (practice theory). This, of course, is my reflection, but it is where I'd like to finish this book—by posing a question for aspiring coaches and leaders to consider:

> *"Could responsive agile coaching, if adopted broadly as a way to have conversations, be a key ingredient in changing an organization's culture and delivering business agility?"*

Aspirations of creating utopia organizations that self-learn have mostly failed due to the practical reality (what people do) not matching the altruistic vision of what Peter Senge called a "Learning Organization." This has led to some academics highlighting the limitations of Senge's attempt to translate the learning organization into a practical theory of organizational change and workplace empowerment. Some even claim it should be abandoned altogether.[2]

I believe the practice-theory gap these academics refer to is agile ways of working and agile coaching conversations. Every agile transformation I know of has had support from agile coaches. They may not have had that as a role title, but the work they did was agile coaching. Having worked in a number of transformation programs, my observation was that the biggest blocker to adoption of agile as a way to work is resistance to change. In other words, people don't want to be told what to do.

Remarkably, the agile coach training and accreditation industry has not dealt with resistance when "certifying" agile coaches. Nearly the entire focus of agile education is on agile theory and practice. There are some providers selling agile leadership training, but coaches are mostly taught technical or process aspects of implementing agile, or the "Tell or Show" move. When a coach meets resistance that requires them to take the down pathway, they are not trained in what move to make in the moment of choice.

The Responsive Agile Coaching model aims to fill this process and practice gap for agile coaches. It is my hope that by equipping themselves to be able to have coaching conversations in the face of resistance, agile coaches will be better able to serve both the client and organization's needs.

To reach the point where agile as a way of working is the norm, everyone needs to be coaching everyone on the way to work and learn; agile coaching needs to be everyone's job. If everyone could facilitate respectful, psychologically safe conversations with each other at all levels of the organization, a true dialogue, then agile as a way of working would have an excellent chance of being embedded as a culture. If we can achieve this, then we have a better chance of creating learning organizations.

Agile Coaching as a Skill

Agile coaching can be done by an agile coach but can also be considered a skill that people can learn. In a recent role I was tasked with teaching employees from across the organization the skill of agile coaching. They had varied backgrounds—from executive assistants, to field workers, to store managers, as well as more traditional roles, such as project managers or scrum masters. Within six months, they were all performing with enough competence that the company stopped recruiting external team coaches and used only internally trained agile coaches to support the hundreds of teams adopting agile for the first time. My point: internally building an agile coaching capability can be and has been done; most people can become (beginner) agile coaches or deliver agile coaching with 6 – 12 months of training, mentoring, and support from expert agile coaches and on-the-job learning.

I'm hoping this book will serve as a manual in what agile coaches need to be taught; this can then be combined with more traditional agile learning and development to produce internal coaches and help agile coaching to be a skill anyone can do.

Coaching Capability for Executives

When considering who to coach and in what order, the topic "What about the execs?" always comes up. When a change to agile is being attempted, it is critical to get the executives on board early (or first). Who I mean by executives are those people with organizational power to effect change. The best way to get them on board is to teach them how to be an exec-as-a-coach. Executives who can coach will understand what a change in mindset actually means from a personal perspective. Of course, executives need training in all the practices of leading with agility, but to quote Ralph Hamers CEO from ING bank who I recently heard talk about their transformation to agile: *"Changing the mindset of leadership is 70 percent of an agile transformation."*

Agile coaches are taught very little on how to help change an executive's mindset. Often the execs sit at round tables and discuss values and principles of agile; they play agile games that are fun and interesting experiences, but when they are back on the job and the pressure to deliver is on, it is the coach who is there to help the exec behave differently. It is my belief that if the Responsive Agile Coaching model was deployed across an organization, it would serve as a means for people to learn how to have open, honest, and transformative conversations about changing the way work gets done. If execs do this first, then it would send a clear and strong signal to all employees that the change to agile is being taken seriously.

When execs demonstrate vulnerability and undergo a transformation of their mindset, it signals to the rest of the organization that a cultural transformation is underway, not just a cost-out or efficiency initiative. The Responsive Agile Coaching model aims to provide a means to support executives through a change in mindset. The model enables deeper conversations; not the coach telling them what to do. If executives can be allowed to co-create the new ways to work, they will be bought in from the start.

My vision for how the Responsive Agile Coaching model could best be deployed would see executives having agile coaching conversations with their agile coach and then conducting coaching conversations themselves with their peers. This is how I've designed the model; to be self-serve and "open sourced," not for exclusive use by those with the title of agile coach but for anyone wishing to deliver agile coaching, regardless of job title.

Chapter Summary

- Aspirational visions for what an organization could look like if it were a self-learning system have been found wanting due to lack of a practice theory to make it happen on the ground. Agile at scale could be considered the missing link to delivering on the promise made by the work of academics such as Peter Senge.

- The "exec as a coach" is a suggested means to ensure executives in an organization experience firsthand the mindset shift required in an agile transformation. If execs were to learn how to conduct responsive agile coaching conversations, it would be one way for them to model the change they want to see across their organization.

- Agile coaching has reached the point where it can be positioned as a skill everyone can learn, not just those with the job title of agile coach. Having agile coaching as a skill allows it to be an enabler of cultural change, reducing the risk of overreliance on a select few agile experts.

References and Further Reading

1. David Dunning, "Chapter Five – The Dunning-Kruger Effect: On Being Ignorant of One's Own Ignorance," *Advances in Experimental Social Psychology* 44, (2011): 247 – 296.

2. Raymond Caldwell, "Systems Thinking, Organizational Change and Agency: A Practice Theory Critique of Senge's Learning Organization," *Journal of Change Management*, (2012): 145 – 164.

3. Go to www.responsiveagile.coach to learn with others who have read or are reading this book; you can also visit www.responsiveagilecoaching.com for up-to-date content, downloads, and templates.

CONCLUSION – FINAL WORDS

sincerely hope this book has both challenged and inspired you. If we truly are in the "age of agile" as Stephen Denning asserts, then we're going to need more than agile coaches to deliver agile coaching. I recently asked a very senior HR leader in a company where I was coaching what message she wanted me to take to the agile community as I presented at an agile conference. She replied, *"Tell all the agile practitioners that there are too few of them and they cost too much."*

This leader was in the middle of spending tens of millions of dollars on agile coaching and was fed up with the lack of agile coaching capability in the market. Why do I mention this? Well, this book aims to provide an open and accessible means to train agile coaching as a skill that anyone can learn; partly solving for the problem the leader was facing as she scrambled to find talent.

One aim I hope I've achieved is to help those with the role title of agile coach to have some more specific details on exactly how to conduct agile coaching conversations; additionally, I also hope this book serves as a guide and reference for those who want to learn agile coaching as a skill.

Of course, this book covers only a part of what has traditionally been seen as an agile coach's set of responsibilities. I haven't specifically covered many important topics, such as facilitation, but what I have done is demystified what agile coaching conversations look like. Once we can see into the parts of an agile coaching conversation, we can then consider how best to master this skill and apply it.

Responsive agile coaching, if delivered well, requires the coach to grow, learn, and become a better human being; a more self-aware, kind, open, and helpful person. I really hope this came out in Steve's story. Personal growth is hard, and there are no shortcuts to excellence. My wish is to make your development journey (a little) easier with this book. For those of you who aspire to grow into agile coaches who specialize in behavior and mindset change, I hope this book serves as your guide.

If we can scale the skill of responsive agile coaching across organizations, I believe it can act as an enabler of broader cultural change when combined with other organizational change activities.

My final comment relates to the promise or vision for what agile was supposed to deliver us. Books have been written and research papers abound on how to create self-learning, responsive organizations utilizing agile values and principles. But agile has mostly failed to deliver on the implied promise of sustainable, healthy, and human work environments that get valuable work DONE. As we continue to uncover better ways of enabling agility by doing it and helping others do it, my hope is that this book's small contribution will move us one step closer to seeing agile finally deliver on what its manifesto declared.